Le Tour de France

Published by Vision Sports Publishing Limited in 2015

Vision Sports Publishing
19-23 High Street
Kingston upon Thames
Surrey
KT1 1LL

www.visionsp.co.uk

© A.S.O. 2015

ISBN: 978-1909534-51-3

Writer: Christian-Louis Éclimont
Translator: Roland Glasser
Editor: Darren Kisner
Design: Zarko Telebak

Le Tour de France 2015

VSP

BY CHRISTIAN PRUDHOMME
TOUR DE FRANCE DIRECTOR

THE MAKER OF LEGENDS

The Tour de France is, above all, about crowning a champion. It was an anxious Froome who mounted his bike before the *pavé* stage to Cambrai; a slightly miffed Froome in Plumelec, where Team Sky had victory snatched from them by BMC by one second; a domineering Froome at La Pierre-Saint-Martin, where his show of strength stunned his rivals, yet didn't smother them; a focussed Froome who crossed the south of France; and finally a relieved Froome following an Alpine campaign marked by the clear erosion of his resources, despite his heading the general classification. Chris Froome's accession to his second Tour title was undertaken at a sure and steady pace, but was far from magisterial. His primary opponent, Nairo Quintana, proved that all of the precautions he had taken in building and managing his time gap were quite justified. The 1'12" that the *maillot jaune* retained following the stunning finale on Alpe d'Huez echoed the time that the Colombian and several other favourites bitterly lost to the wind in Zeeland — something to think about for the future.

Beyond the effort made by Quintana to unseat Froome, the three weeks of racing also provided a rich tapestry of life; with smiles, tears and all kinds of emotion. The road was indomitable, and at times even cruel to the yellow jersey when worn by Fabian Cancellara and Tony Martin. But it also served as a springboard for ambition in the case of Alexis Vuillermoz, or provided an unexpected sparkle to the destiny of Simon Geschke, the German cyclist who was a surprise winner at Pra-Loup.

And this monumental and unpredictable maker of legends that is the Tour de France also created new and exciting episodes in the saga of French cycling, which has been somewhat disillusioned and browbeaten of late. With a mixture of pride and romanticism, the vanguard of the new generation distinguished themselves by inspired, powerful demonstrations of prowess, in Saint-Jean-de-Maurienne for Romain Bardet, and on Alpe d'Huez for Thibaut Pinot, while Warren Barguil had a clear message: "I now know I'm a Grand Tour cyclist" — he could have been speaking for all of them.

TEAMS

 ASTANA PRO TEAM (KAZ)

1. Vincenzo NIBALI (ITA)
2. Lars BOOM (NED)
3. Jakob FUGLSANG (DEN)
4. Andriy GRIVKO (UKR)
5. Dmitriy GRUZDEV (KAZ)
6. Tanel KANGERT (EST)
7. Michele SCARPONI (ITA)
8. Rein TAARAMÄE (EST)
9. Lieuwe WESTRA (NED)

 TEAM SKY (GBR)

31. Christopher FROOME (GBR)
32. Peter KENNAUGH (GBR)
33. Leopold KÖNIG (CZE)
34. Wouter POELS (NED)
35. Richie PORTE (AUS)
36. Nicolas ROCHE (IRL)
37. Luke ROWE (GBR)
38. Ian STANNARD (GBR)
39. Geraint THOMAS (GBR)

 BMC RACING TEAM (USA)

61. Tejay VAN GARDEREN (USA)
62. Damiano CARUSO (ITA)
63. Rohan DENNIS (AUS)
64. Daniel OSS (ITA)
65. Manuel QUINZIATO (ITA)
66. Samuel SÁNCHEZ (ESP)
67. Michael SCHÄR (SUI)
68. Greg VAN AVERMAET (BEL)
69. Danilo WYSS (SUI)

 TEAM KATUSHA (RUS)

91. Joaquim RODRÍGUEZ (ESP)
92. Gianpaolo CARUSO (ITA)
93. Jacopo GUARNIERI (ITA)
94. Marco HALLER (AUT)
95. Dmitry KOZONTCHUK (RUS)
96. Alexander KRISTOFF (NOR)
97. Alberto LOSADA (ESP)
98. Tiago MACHADO (POR)
99. Luca PAOLINI (ITA)

 AG2R LA MONDIALE (FRA)

11. Jean-Christophe PÉRAUD (FRA)
12. Romain BARDET (FRA)
13. Jan BAKELANTS (BEL)
14. Mikaël CHEREL (FRA)
15. Ben GASTAUER (LUX)
16. Damien GAUDIN (FRA)
17. Christophe RIBLON (FRA)
18. Johan VANSUMMEREN (BEL)
19. Alexis VUILLERMOZ (FRA)

 TINKOFF-SAXO (RUS)

41. Alberto CONTADOR (ESP)
42. Ivan BASSO (ITA)
43. Daniele BENNATI (ITA)
44. Roman KREUZIGER (CZE)
45. Rafał MAJKA (POL)
46. Michael ROGERS (AUS)
47. Peter SAGAN (SVK)
48. Matteo TOSATTO (ITA)
49. Michael VALGREN (DEN)

 LOTTO-SOUDAL (BEL)

71. Tony GALLOPIN (FRA)
72. Lars BAK (DEN)
73. Thomas DE GENDT (BEL)
74. Jens DEBUSSCHERE (BEL)
75. André GREIPEL (GER)
76. Adam HANSEN (AUS)
77. Gregory HENDERSON (NZL)
78. Marcel SIEBERG (GER)
79. Tim WELLENS (BEL)

 ORICA-GREENEDGE (AUS)

101. Simon GERRANS (AUS)
102. Michael ALBASINI (SUI)
103. Luke DURBRIDGE (AUS)
104. Daryl IMPEY (RSA)
105. Michael MATTHEWS (AUS)
106. Svein TUFT (CAN)
107. Pieter WEENING (NED)
108. Adam YATES (GBR)
109. Simon YATES (GBR)

 FDJ (FRA)

21. Thibaut PINOT (FRA)
22. William BONNET (FRA)
23. Sébastien CHAVANEL (FRA)
24. Arnaud DÉMARE (FRA)
25. Alexandre GENIEZ (FRA)
26. Matthieu LADAGNOUS (FRA)
27. Steve MORABITO (SUI)
28. Jérémy ROY (FRA)
29. Benoît VAUGRENARD (FRA)

 MOVISTAR TEAM (ESP)

51. Nairo QUINTANA (COL)
52. Winner ANACONA (COL)
53. Jonathan CASTROVIEJO (ESP)
54. Alex DOWSETT (GBR)
55. Imanol ERVITI (ESP)
56. José HERRADA (ESP)
57. Gorka IZAGIRRE (ESP)
58. Adriano MALORI (ITA)
59. Alejandro VALVERDE (ESP)

 TEAM GIANT-ALPECIN (GER)

81. John DEGENKOLB (GER)
82. Warren BARGUIL (FRA)
83. Roy CURVERS (NED)
84. Koen DE KORT (NED)
85. Tom DUMOULIN (NED)
86. Simon GESCHKE (GER)
87. Georg PREIDLER (AUT)
88. Ramon SINKELDAM (NED)
89. Albert TIMMER (NED)

 ETIXX — QUICK-STEP (BEL)

111. Michał KWIATKOWSKI (POL)
112. Mark CAVENDISH (GBR)
113. Michał GOLAS (POL)
114. Tony MARTIN (GER)
115. Mark RENSHAW (AUS)
116. Zdeněk ŠTYBAR (CZE)
117. Matteo TRENTIN (ITA)
118. Rigoberto URÁN (COL)
119. Julien VERMOTE (BEL)

TEAM EUROPCAR (FRA)

121. Pierre ROLLAND (FRA)
122. Bryan COQUARD (FRA)
123. Cyril GAUTIER (FRA)
124. Yohann GÈNE (FRA)
125. Bryan NAULLEAU (FRA)
126. Perrig QUÉMÉNEUR (FRA)
127. Romain SICARD (FRA)
128. Angélo TULIK (FRA)
129. Thomas VOECKLER (FRA)

LAMPRE-MERIDA (ITA)

151. Rui COSTA (POR)
152. Matteo BONO (ITA)
153. Davide CIMOLAI (ITA)
154. Kristijan ĐURASEK (CRO)
155. Nelson OLIVEIRA (POR)
156. Rubén PLAZA (ESP)
157. Filippo POZZATO (ITA)
158. José SERPA (COL)
159. Rafael VALLS (ESP)

IAM CYCLING (SUI)

181. Mathias FRANK (SUI)
182. Matthias BRÄNDLE (AUT)
183. Sylvain CHAVANEL (FRA)
184. Stef CLEMENT (NED)
185. Jérôme COPPEL (FRA)
186. Martin ELMIGER (SUI)
187. Reto HOLLENSTEIN (SUI)
188. Jarlinson PANTANO (COL)
189. Marcel WYSS (SUI)

MTN-QHUBEKA (RSA)

211. Edvald BOASSON HAGEN (NOR)
212. Stephen CUMMINGS (GBR)
213. Tyler FARRAR (USA)
214. Jacques JANSE VAN RENSBURG (RSA)
215. Reinardt JANSE VAN RENSBURG (RSA)
216. Merhawi KUDUS (ERI)
217. Louis MEINTJES (RSA)
218. Serge PAUWELS (BEL)
219. Daniel TEKLEHAIMANOT (ERI)

TEAM LOTTO NL-JUMBO (NED)

131. Robert GESINK (NED)
132. Wilco KELDERMAN (NED)
133. Steven KRUIJSWIJK (NED)
134. Thomas LEEZER (NED)
135. Paul MARTENS (GER)
136. Bram TANKINK (NED)
137. Laurens TEN DAM (NED)
138. Jos VAN EMDEN (NED)
139. Sep VANMARCKE (BEL)

TEAM CANNONDALE-GARMIN (USA)

161. Andrew TALANSKY (USA)
162. Jack BAUER (NZL)
163. Nathan HAAS (USA)
164. Ryder HESJEDAL (USA)
165. Kristijan KOREN (SVK)
166. Sebastian LANGEVELD (NED)
167. Daniel MARTIN (IRL)
168. Ramūnas NAVARDAUSKAS (LIT)
169. Dylan VAN BAARLE (NED)

BORA-ARGON 18 (GER)

191. Dominik NERZ (GER)
192. Jan BARTA (CZE)
193. Sam BENNETT (IRL)
194. Emanuel BUCHMANN (GER)
195. Zakkari DEMPSTER (AUS)
196. Bartosz HUZARSKI (POL)
197. José MENDES (POR)
198. Andreas SCHILLINGER (GER)
199. Paul VOSS (GER)

TREK FACTORY RACING (USA)

141. Bauke MOLLEMA (NED)
142. Julián ARREDONDO MORENO (COL)
143. Fabian CANCELLARA (SUI)
144. Stijn DEVOLDER (BEL)
145. Laurent DIDIER (LUX)
146. Markel IRIZAR (ESP)
147. Bob JUNGELS (LUX)
148. Grégory RAST (SUI)
149. Haimar ZUBELDIA (ESP)

COFIDIS, SOLUTIONS CRÉDITS (FRA)

171. Nacer BOUHANNI (FRA)
172. Nicolas EDET (FRA)
173. Christophe LAPORTE (FRA)
174. Luis Ángel MATÉ (ESP)
175. Daniel NAVARRO (ESP)
176. Florian SÉNÉCHAL (FRA)
177. Julien SIMON (FRA)
178. Geoffrey SOUPE (FRA)
179. Kenneth VANBILSEN (BEL)

BRETAGNE-SÉCHÉ ENVIRONNEMENT (FRA)

201. Eduardo SEPÚLVEDA (ARG)
202. Fréderic BRUN (FRA)
203. Anthony DELAPLACE (FRA)
204. Pierrick FÉDRIGO (FRA)
205. Brice FEILLU (FRA)
206. Armindo FONSECA (FRA)
207. Arnaud GÉRARD (FRA)
208. Pierre-Luc PÉRICHON (FRA)
209. Florian VACHON (FRA)

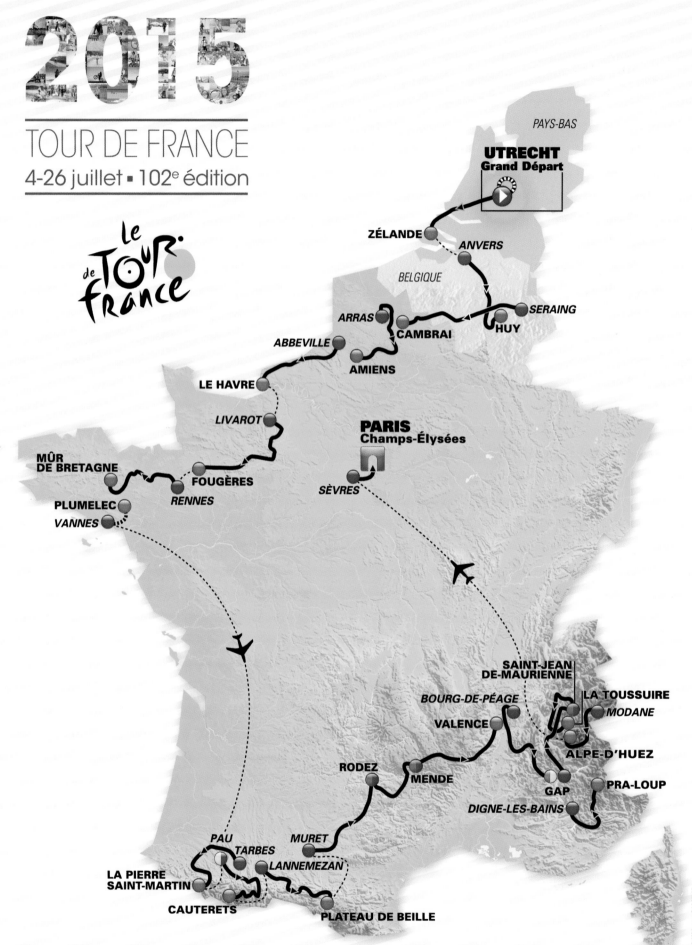

2015

TOUR DE FRANCE
4-26 juillet ▪ 102ᵉ édition

le de TOUR France

PAYS-BAS

UTRECHT
Grand Départ

ZÉLANDE

ANVERS

BELGIQUE

SERAING

ARRAS

CAMBRAI

HUY

ABBEVILLE

AMIENS

LE HAVRE

LIVAROT

PARIS
Champs-Élysées

MÛR DE BRETAGNE

FOUGÈRES

RENNES

PLUMELEC

SÈVRES

VANNES

SAINT-JEAN DE-MAURIENNE

BOURG-DE-PÉAGE

LA TOUSSUIRE

MODANE

VALENCE

ALPE-D'HUEZ

RODEZ

MENDE

PRA-LOUP

GAP

DIGNE-LES-BAINS

PAU

MURET

TARBES

LANNEMEZAN

LA PIERRE SAINT-MARTIN

CAUTERETS

PLATEAU DE BEILLE

LÉGENDE / THE KEY

- ◉ Grand Départ — Race Start
- ⬤ Ville départ — Start town
- ◯ Ville repos — Rest town
- ⫿⫿⫿ C.l.m. individuel — Individual time trial
- ▯ Arrivée finale — Race Finish
- ⬤ Ville arrivée — Finish town
- ▬ Étape en ligne — Stage
- ⦙⦙⦙⦙ C.l.m. par équipe — Team time trial

©A.S.O 2014 - GEOATLAS.com

CONTENTS

12   STAGE 1   Saturday 4 July   **UTRECHT (NED) > UTRECHT, INDIVIDUAL TIME TRIAL – 13.8 KM**

18   TOUR HISTORY   **THE GRANDS DÉPARTS OUTSIDE FRANCE**

22   STAGE 2   Sunday 5 July   **UTRECHT (NED) > ZEELAND (NED) – 166 KM**

26   STAGE 3   Monday 6 July   **ANTWERP (BEL) > HUY (BEL) – 159.5 KM**

30   STAGE 4   Tuesday 7 July   **SERAING (BEL) > CAMBRAI (FRA) – 223.5 KM**

36   TOUR HISTORY   **COBBLES ON THE TOUR**

38   STAGE 5   Wednesday 8 July   **ARRAS > AMIENS – 189.5 KM**

42   STAGE 6   Thursday 9 July   **ABBEVILLE > LE HAVRE – 191.5 KM**

48   STAGE 7   Friday 10 July   **LIVAROT > FOUGÈRES – 190.5 KM**

52   TOUR HISTORY   **THE TOUR IN BRITTANY**

54   STAGE 8   Saturday 11 July   **RENNES > MÛR-DE-BRETAGNE – 181.5 KM**

58   STAGE 9   Sunday 12 July   **VANNES > PLUMELEC, TEAM TIME TRIAL – 28 KM**

62   STAGE 10   Tuesday 14 July   **TARBES > LA PIERRE-SAINT-MARTIN – 167 KM**

66   STAGE 11   Wednesday 15 July   **PAU > CAUTERETS – 188 KM**

72   STAGE 12   Thursday 16 July   **LANNEMEZAN > PLATEAU DE BEILLE – 195 KM**

78   TOUR HISTORY   **THE WHITE JERSEY**

80   STAGE 13   Friday 17 July   **MURET > RODEZ – 198.5 KM**

84   STAGE 14   Saturday 18 July   **RODEZ > MENDE – 178.5 KM**

90   STAGE 15   Sunday 19 July   **MENDE > VALENCE – 183 KM**

94   STAGE 16   Monday 20 July   **BOURG-DE-PÉAGE > GAP – 201 KM**

104   STAGE 17   Wednesday 22 July   **DIGNE-LES-BAINS > PRA-LOUP – 161 KM**

108   TOUR HISTORY   **THE POLKA DOT JERSEY**

110   STAGE 18   Thursday 23 July   **GAP > SAINT-JEAN-DE-MAURIENNE – 186.5 KM**

116   STAGE 19   Friday 24 July   **SAINT-JEAN-DE-MAURIENNE > LA TOUSSUIRE – 138 KM**

122   STAGE 20   Saturday 25 July   **MODANE VALFRÉJUS > ALPE D'HUEZ – 110.5 KM**

128   TOUR HISTORY   **THE LEGENDARY ALPE D'HUEZ**

132   STAGE 21   Sunday 26 July   **SÈVRES > PARIS CHAMPS-ÉLYSÉES – 109.5 KM**

138   TOUR HISTORY   **FORTY YEARS ON THE CHAMPS-ÉLYSÉES**

142   **FINAL CLASSIFICATIONS**

1. At the rider presentation in Utrecht, Chris Froome and the rest of the Sky team have their sights set on glory.

2. With nine Tour victories between them, from left to right: Jan Janssen, Bernard Hinault, Joop Zoetemelk and Bernard Thévenet.

3. Thibaut Pinot was third overall in the 2014 Tour, as well as winning the best young rider competition. He looks on top form for this year's race.

4. Vincenzo Nibali, Astana team leader and winner of the 2014 Tour de France, seems to be under no pressure at all.

5. In a country where bicycles rule, the town of Utrecht has gone all out to celebrate the Tour de France.

6. "From the first to the last, champions all" — these spectators would certainly agree!

7. MTN-Qhubeka (South Africa) is the first African registered team to ride in the Tour de France.

8. The polka dot jersey is forty years old this year. They may not have mountains in the Netherlands, but that doesn't stop the celebrations.

Twenty-five year old Australian rider Rohan Dennis, who won the Tour Down Under at the start of the season, steps into the limelight wearing yellow.

ROHAN DENNIS, A RECORD-BREAKING RIDE INTO YELLOW

A t two o'clock on the dot, the Eritrean rider Daniel Teklehaimanot rolled down the starting ramp and into the history books. His team, MTN-Qhubeka, is based in South Africa, and is the first African registered team to ride in the Tour de France. Ahead of him lay the first stage of the 2015 Tour: a 13.8 km individual time trial through the town of Utrecht, where sinuous stretches alternated with long straights, under the baking summer sun. This was a course perfectly suited to time trial specialists — experts at shooting through the tightest turns with the minimum loss of speed, and at digging deep to find that extra turn of the pedal where it counts.

Of course, all eyes were on the "fantastic four", widely considered to be the favourites: Chris Froome, Alberto Contador, Vincenzo Nibali and Nairo Quintana. They all finished within 17 seconds of each other, in the top half of the leader board. As for the French riders tipped to do well in this year's race, Thibaut Pinot excelled himself. He finished in eighteenth place, at 41", which made up for his less than satisfactory performance in the final stage time trial at the recent Tour of Switzerland. Jean-Christophe Péraud managed a reasonably respectable fiftieth place, at 59", while Romain Bardet came in at 1'34".

The Dutch riders were determined not to come up short on home soil, and several did their country proud. Most notable was Tom Dumoulin, who fulfilled the promise of his superb time trialling results earlier in the season by finishing fourth, at 8". He rolled in just ahead of his compatriots Jos van Emden, in fifth place, and Wilco Kelderman, in ninth.

But the surprise of the day was served up by the Australian Rohan Dennis, who managed to keep time trial veterans Tony Martin and Fabian Cancellara off the top spot, not to mention set a new record for the fastest average speed in a Tour de France time trial: a blistering 55.446 km/h. Martin seemed to suffer from the heat on the second part of the course, while Cancellara, perhaps still not entirely recovered from his serious crash in March, couldn't rise sufficiently to the occasion, despite his characteristically powerful pedalling style.

Rohan Dennis embodies the new generation of Australian road cyclists who learned their trade on the track. Joining the BMC Racing Team in August 2014, Dennis straightaway helped the squad to victory in the World Team Time Trial Championships in September. He then went on to set a new hour record on February 8 2015 at the Granges Velodrome in Switzerland, covering 52.491 kilometres. His early potential now decisively confirmed, Rohan Dennis is clearly a man to watch. ∎

> *"To wear the Tour de France yellow jersey, it's a dream. I always wanted to be in this position and now I am."*
> **ROHAN DENNIS**

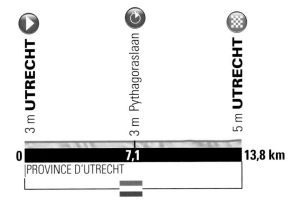

GENERAL CLASSIFICATION AFTER STAGE 1

1. DENNIS Rohan (AUS, BMC) 14'56"
2. Martin T (GER, Etixx – Quick-Step) +5"
3. Cancellara F (SUI, Trek) +6"
4. Dumoulin T (NED, Giant-Alpecin) +8"
5. van Emden J (NED, LottoNL-Jumbo) +15"
6. Castroviejo J (ESP, Movistar) +23"
7. Brändle M (AUT, IAM) +23"
8. Malori A (ITA, Movistar) +29"
9. Kelderman W (NED, LottoNL-Jumbo) +30"
10. Cummings S (GBR, MTN-Qhubeka) +32"
11. Gesink R (NED, LottoNL-Jumbo) +33"
12. Thomas G (GBR, Sky) +33"
13. Dowsett A (GBR, Movistar) +36"
14. Mollema B (NED, Trek) +37"
15. Jungels B (NED, Trek) +38"

Winner's average speed: 55.446 km/h

DENNIS R (AUS, BMC)

DENNIS R (AUS, BMC)
worn by T. Martin

DENNIS R (AUS, BMC)
worn by T. Dumoulin

Team classification

TEAM LOTTO NL-JUMBO:
46'06"

(Top) Local hero, Tom Dumoulin finishes fourth in the individual time trial in Utrecht, making him the highest placed Dutch rider. (Bottom) Resplendent in the German Time Trial Champion's jersey with World Champion's stripes, thirty-year-old Tony Martin finished a close second.

With an average speed of
55.446 km/h, Rohan Dennis broke
the record set by Chris Boardman
(55.152 km/h) during the
7.2 km prologue in Lille, 1994.

Back in action, after his spring classics
campaign was ended by a crash
at the E3 Harelbeke, Fabian Cancellara
puts in a Herculean ride to place third
in the first stage of the 2015 Tour.

A TRADITION DATING BACK TO THE 1950s

Between 1903, when the Tour de France began, and 1936, this epic cycling race experienced a period of constant change and innovation, under the iron rod of its stern founder and boss, Henri Desgranges. He was always ready to tweak the regulations to keep things interesting and ensure heightened suspense for the spectators. It was an obsession that sometimes ended up triggering a revolt on the part of the cyclists or astonishment from the journalists, who did not always appreciate the impact of his fastidious tinkering. In his defence, he was merely moulding a sporting event against a background of considerable change. In 1910, one of his main concerns was the threat from mountain bears on the Peyresourde. By 1929, it was the explosion of media, chiefly radio, which preoccupied him.

After the Second World War, Jacques Goddet, (Desgranges' successor, appointed in 1936), aware of the spectacular impact of the race internationally, brought some stability to the Tour's foundations. With the creation of the Council of Europe in 1949, Europe began to forge a new future, and so did the Tour. On 8 July 1954, the Grand Départ of the forty-first edition of the race was held outside France for the first time. This first stage, from Amsterdam to Brasschaat in Belgium, was 216 kilometres long, and was won by a Dutch national, Wout Wagtmans, who took the yellow jersey twice during the tour and held it for a total of seven days. Louison Bobet was the race's overall winner, Frederico Bahamontès was crowned best climber, Ferdi Kubler took the points jersey and Switzerland won the team competition. A tradition was established, and by 2015, the Tour had staged twenty-one Grands Départs abroad.

To date, the Netherlands tops the leader board with six Grands Départs, ahead of Belgium's four, including two in Liège (2004 and 2012), and Germany's three, with the memorable West Berlin stage of 1987, two years before the Wall came down. Luxembourg has hosted two, both in its capital, as has the United Kingdom, in London (2007) and Leeds (2014), while Spain, Ireland, Monaco and Switzerland have hosted one each. The Netherlands also leads when it comes to home winners of foreign Grands Départs. After Wout Wagtmans' success in 1954, Joop Zoetemelk won at Scheveningen in 1973 and Jan Raas was victorious at Leiden in 1978. Spain follows with Miguel Indurain, who took the stage at San Sébastian in 1992. With the exception of Wagtmans's, all these victories were achieved in prologues.

The specialist and record-holder of Grand Départ wins is of course Fabian Cancellara. He brought honour to his native Switzerland between 2004 and 2012 by winning five times: in Liège (2004 and 2012), London (2007), Monaco (2009) and Rotterdam (2010). It's worth noting that of the twenty Grands Départs held outside France, only three were mass-start stages, all of which were won in sprints: Brussels to Ghent (1958), won by Frenchman André Darrigade; Cologne to Liège (1965), won by the Belgian Rik Van Looy; and Leeds to Harrogate (2014), in which the German Marcel Kittel claimed victory.

> *The original motivation behind these occasional adventures abroad was a sporting one, born of a desire to honour the nations whose cyclists made such a huge contribution to the Tour's legendary status.*

TOUR DE FRANCE 1954
Final preparations are made
for the Grand Départ in Amsterdam's
Olympic Stadium.

Holding Grands Départs outside France was a popular trend in the 1970s and '80s, with four in nine years: Scheveningen (1973), Charleroi (1975), Leiden (1978) and Frankfurt (1980). It returned to vogue in the 2010s with three in just four years: Liège (2012), Leeds (2014) and Utrecht (2015). The original motivation behind these occasional adventures abroad was a sporting one, born of a desire to honour the nations whose cyclists made such a huge contribution to the Tour's legendary status. The reality today is that they also help to promote France's organisational *savoir faire* and reinforce its national prestige, which translates into a boost for tourism across the whole country. ■

THE GRANDS DÉPARTS OUTSIDE FRANCE

1954 1st stage | Amsterdam (NED) > Brasschaat (BEL) | 216 km | Winner: Wout Wagtmans (NED)
1958 1st stage | Brussels (BEL) > Ghent (BEL) | 184 km | Winner: André Darrigade (FRA)
1965 1st stage | Cologne (FRG) > Liège (BEL) | 149 km | Winner: Rik Van Looy (BEL)
1973 Prologue | Scheveningen (NED) | 7.1 km (ITT) | Winner: Joop Zoetemelk (NED)
1975 Prologue | Charleroi (BEL) | 6.25 km (ITT) | Winner: Francesco Moser (ITA)
1978 Prologue | Leiden (NED) | 5.2 km (ITT) | Winner: Jan Raas (NED)
1980 Prologue | Frankfurt (FRG) | 7.6 km (ITT) | Winner: Bernard Hinault (FRA)
1982 Prologue | Basle (SUI) | 7.4 km (ITT) | Winner: Bernard Hinault (FRA)
1987 Prologue | West Berlin (FRG) | 6.1 km (ITT) | Winner: Jelle Nijdam (NED)
1989 Prologue | Luxembourg (LUX) | 7.8 km (ITT) | Winner: Erik Breukink (NED)
1992 Prologue | San Sebastián (ESP) | 8 km (ITT) | Winner: Miguel Indurain (ESP)
1996 Prologue | 's-Hertogenbosch (NED) | 9.4 km (ITT) | Winner: Alex Zülle (SUI)
1998 Prologue | Dublin (IRL) | 5.6 km (ITT) | Winner: Chris Boardman (GBR)
2002 Prologue | Luxembourg (LUX) | 6.5 km (ITT) | Winner: Lance Armstrong (USA)
2004 Prologue | Liège (BEL) | 6.1 km (ITT) | Winner: Fabian Cancellara (SUI)
2007 Prologue | London (GBR) | 7.9 km (ITT) | Winner: Fabian Cancellara (SUI)
2009 1st stage | Monaco (MON) | 15.5 km (ITT) | Winner: Fabian Cancellara (SUI)
2010 Prologue | Rotterdam (NED) | 8.9 km (ITT) | Winner: Fabian Cancellara (SUI)
2012 Prologue | Liège (BEL) | 6.4 km (ITT) | Winner: Fabian Cancellara (SUI)
2014 1st stage | Leeds (GBR) > Harrogate (GBR) | 190.5 km | Winner: Marcel Kittel (GER)

(MAIN PICTURE)
TOUR DE FRANCE 1987
Berlin welcomed the Tour over two days (1 and 2 July) for a prologue and two stages: the first was a mass-start stage, the second a team time trial. The Dutch rider Jelle Nijdam won the prologue, while his countryman Nico Verhoeven took stage one. The Italian Carrera team triumphed in the TTT.

(INSET)
TOUR DE FRANCE 2014
Huge crowds line the roads from Leeds to Harrogate, cheering the peloton as it tackles the steep climbs of the Yorkshire Dales, for what was described by Tour Director Christian Prudhomme as the "grandest" of Grands Départs.

A skilful bike-handler, with power to match, André Greipel beats Peter Sagan, Fabian Cancellara and Mark Cavendish to the line in Zeeland.

ANDRÉ GREIPEL
POWERS TO VICTORY

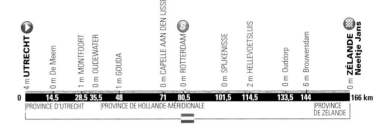

It is a Tour paradox that a pancake-flat stage can sometimes serve up more drama than a mountainous one. This is what happened on the road from Utrecht to Zeeland, a peninsula where the wind reigns supreme. As stormy weather battered the riders, nervousness spread through the peloton.

To make sure their leader stayed out of trouble, Alberto Contador's Tinkoff-Saxo team assumed pole position and put the hammer down. As they entered the province of South Holland, 40 km from the finish, a combination of their pounding pace and a change in wind direction caused a split in the peloton that dealt a substantial blow to several of the favourites. Vincenzo Nibali, Nairo Quintana, Thibaut Pinot and Rohan Dennis were all caught on the wrong side of the break. Chris Froome, along with Tejay van Garderen, Peter Sagan, Mark Cavendish, André Greipel, Tony Martin and Fabian Cancellara all managed to stay hitched to the Tinkoff-Saxo train.

It was no great surprise that Rohan Dennis — the freshly minted maillot jaune — would relinquish his leader's jersey by the end of a stage that was never likely to suit him. Nibali and Quintana, on the other hand, could never have dreamed that they would lose nearly a minute and a half on their main rivals.

The success of the Tinkoff-Saxo offensive was in no small measure aided by the collusion of the indefatigable German, Tony Martin, who longed to exchange his green points jersey for yellow. As for Cavendish, he had his sights set on re-opening his ledger of Tour victories, which stood at twenty-five. But the Manx Missile launched too soon, pulling André Greipel along in his slipstream. The Gorilla from Rostock roared past to claim victory — his eleventh of the season — beating Peter Sagan into second place by the narrowest of margins.

Fabian Cancellara, meanwhile, also had his heart set on winning the yellow jersey, for the twenty-ninth time in his career. To achieve that, he needed to close a six second gap on the GC leader, which meant mixing it up in the sprint. This he did in superb style, throwing his bike across the line to claim third place, barely a wheel rim ahead of Cavendish. A four second bonus was enough to carry him into yellow, depriving Tony Martin of the top spot once again.

The ever vigilant Chris Froome finished in the lead bunch, managing to gain an extra four seconds on Alberto Contador in the last few hundred metres. Nevertheless, it was a good day for both riders, catching the wind and stealing a march on their rivals. But no doubt they realised that every stage of the Tour de France is a new chapter, and luck, like the wind, can change. ∎

> ## *"Cavendish went too soon. When I saw Sagan pull out, I knew it was the right moment."*
> **ANDRÉ GREIPEL**

CLASSIFICATION FOR STAGE 2

1. GREIPEL André (GER, Lotto-Soudal) 3h29'03"
2. Sagan P (SVK, Tinkoff-Saxo) +0"
3. Cancellara F (SUI, Trek) +0"
4. Cavendish M (GBR, Etixx – Quick-Step) +0"
5. Oss D (ITA, BMC) +0"
6. Van Avermaet G (BEL, BMC) +0"
7. Froome C (GBR, Sky) +0"
8. Dumoulin T (NED, Giant-Alpecin) +0"
9. Martin T (GER, Etixx – Quick-Step) +0"
10. Barguil W (FRA, Giant-Alpecin) +0"
11. van Garderen T (USA, BMC) +4"
12. Thomas G (GBR, Sky) +4"
13. Contador A (ESP, Tinkoff-Saxo) +4"
14. Urán R (COL, Etixx – Quick-Step) +4"
15. Gallopin T (FRA, Lotto-Soudal) +4"

Winner's average speed: 47.6 km/h

GENERAL CLASSIFICATION

1. CANCELLARA Fabian (SUI, Trek) 3h44'01"
2. Martin T (GER, Etixx – Quick-Step) +3"
3. Dumoulin T (NED, Giant-Alpecin) +6"
4. Sagan P (SVK, Tinkoff-Saxo) +33"
5. Thomas G (GBR, Sky) +35"
6. Oss D (ITA, BMC) +42"
7. Urán R (COL, Etixx – Quick-Step) +42"
8. van Garderen T (USA, BMC) +44"
9. Van Avermaet G (BEL, BMC) +48"
10. Froome C (GBR, Sky) +48"
11. Rogers M (AUS, Tinkoff-Saxo) +53"
12. Štybar Z (CZE, Etixx – Quick-Step) +54"
13. Greipel A (GER, Lotto-Soudal) +59"
14. Contador A (ESP, Tinkoff-Saxo) +1'
15. Gallopin T (FRA, Lotto-Soudal) +1'

CANCELLARA F
(SUI, TREK)

GREIPEL A
(GER, LOTTO-SOUDAL)

DUMOULIN T
(NED, GIANT-ALPECIN)

Team classification

BMC RACING TEAM:
11h13'27"

MOST AGGRESSIVE RIDER
KWIATKOWSKI M (POL, ETIXX – QUICK-STEP)

The formation of echelons in the peloton is a sure sign that the riders are in for a hard afternoon fighting the elements.

(Top) Caught out by a split in the peloton, Thibaut Pinot (right) finds himself nearly 1'30" behind the lead group. (Bottom) The teams of GC contenders, Contador (Tinkoff-Saxo), van Garderen (BMC) and Froome (Sky), work hard to put as much time as possible between themselves and the other favourites.

A jubilant Joaquim Rodríguez savours his second Tour stage victory, following his win at Mende in 2010, and takes the polka dot jersey.

JOAQUIM RODRÍGUEZ CONQUERS THE CARNAGE

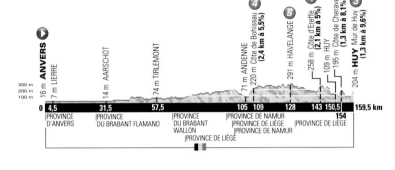

At four o'clock in the afternoon, the tightly-packed peloton was hurtling down a long, straight, slightly descending stretch of road, when William Bonnet of Française des Jeux clipped a wheel and went tumbling, triggering a pile-up of more than twenty riders. They skidded and somersaulted along the road and into the ditch in a chaotic whirl of limbs and bicycles. In the aftermath, the unfortunate Bonnet lay tattered on the tarmac, his injuries forcing his immediate withdrawal from the race, along with Tom Dumoulin, Simon Gerrans and Dmitry Kozontchuk.

Even the *maillot jaune* was not spared this cataclysm. Fabian Cancellara found himself sprawled on the Belgian verge, barely 100 km from the spot where he had crashed heavily three months earlier during the E3 Harelbeke. Moments later, a second crash brought down another twenty riders. While medics and mechanics untangled bikes and bodies, the now 120-strong peloton disappeared into the distance. With all four ambulances and both medical cars fully occupied, Tour director Christian Prudhomme felt he had no choice but to neutralise the race. His car was soon surrounded by a gaggle of angry riders desperate to continue racing. But his decision was the most sensible; to carry on without medical assistance would have been dangerous. It was also the most sporting, allowing those riders involved in the crashes to receive first aid and, in most cases, rejoin the waiting peloton.

At 4.23 pm, the race was restarted at the top of the Côte de Bohissau — for which no points were awarded for the mountains classification. Drained of adrenaline, the peloton took a little while to get back into race mode, but soon Tinkoff-Saxo were setting a blistering pace. As the hills around Huy came into sight, most of the favourites were positioned towards the front of the pack, ready to do battle on the *Mur*, famous finale of the spring classic, La Flèche-Wallonne. At just over 1 km, with gradients of up to 26%, the Wall of Huy is a fitting name for this final stretch.

About 500 metres from the line, Joaquim Rodríguez launched his attack. Tony Gallopin stuck to his wheel, initially outpacing Chris Froome. But as the gradient ramped up, the Frenchman faded, leaving Froome to pursue Rodríguez up the grindingly steep slope. Gritting his teeth, the Spaniard held off the Sky man to win the stage, with Froome picking up a "consolation prize": the *maillot jaune*. Nibali, Quintana and Valverde finished at 11" and Contador at 18". Thibaut Pinot limped home at 1'33", and Cancellara, clearly suffering after his fall, rolled in over 11 minutes down. It had been a long, painful day for many. And with the hell of the *pavé* looming, there would be little respite for weary, battered bodies. ■

> *"Honestly, this felt like the longest climb of the Mur de Huy I've ever done."*
>
> **JOAQUIM RODRÍGUEZ**

CLASSIFICATION FOR STAGE 3

1. RODRÍGUEZ Joaquim (ESP, Katusha) 3h26'54"
2. Froome C (GBR, Sky) +0"
3. Vuillermoz A (FRA, AG2R) +4"
4. Martin D (IRL, Cannondale-Garmin) +5"
5. Gallopin T (FRA, Lotto-Soudal) +8"
6. van Garderen T (USA, BMC) +11"
7. Nibali V (ITA, Astana) +11"
8. Yates S (GBR, Orica-GreenEdge) +11"
9. Quintana N (COL, Movistar) +11"
10. Mollema B (NED, Trek) +11"
11. Valverde A (ESP, Movistar) +11"
12. Contador A (ESP, Tinkoff-Saxo) +18"
13. Arredondo J (COL, Trek) +19"
14. Gesink R (NED, LottoNL-Jumbo) +22"
15. Van Avermaet G (BEL, BMC) +22"

Winner's average speed: 46.3 km/h
Did not finish: Gerrans S (AUS, Orica-GreenEdge), Kozontchuk D (RUS, Katusha), Dumoulin T (NED, Giant-Alpecin), Bonnet W (FRA, FDJ)

GENERAL CLASSIFICATION

1. FROOME Christopher (GBR, Sky) 7h11'37"
2. Martin T (GER, Etixx – Quick-Step) +1"
3. van Garderen T (USA, BMC) +13"
4. Gallopin T (FRA, Lotto-Soudal) +26"
5. Van Avermaet G (BEL, BMC) +28"
6. Sagan P (SVK, Tinkoff-Saxo) +31"
7. Urán R (COL, Etixx – Quick-Step) +34"
8. Contador A (ESP, Tinkoff-Saxo) +36"
9. Thomas G (GBR, Sky) +1'03"
10. Štybar Z (CZE, Etixx – Quick-Step) +1'04"
11. Barguil W (FRA, Giant-Alpecin) +1'07"
12. Mollema B (NED, Trek) +1'32"
13. Nibali V (ITA, Astana) +1'38"
14. Gesink R (NED, LottoNL-Jumbo) +1'39"
15. Kreuziger R (CZE, Tinkoff-Saxo) +1'51"

FROOME C
(GBR, SKY)

GREIPEL A
(GER, LOTTO-SOUDAL)

RODRÍGUEZ J
(ESP, KATUSHA)

SAGAN P
(SVK, TINKOFF-SAXO)

Team classification

BMC RACING TEAM:
21h35'52"

MOST AGGRESSIVE RIDER
BARTA J (CZE, BORA-ARGON 18)

(Top) The race is neutralised after a massive crash, just 50 km from the finish. (Bottom) The agony of the *maillot jaune*. Fabian Cancellara winces in pain, as the race prepares to restart.

Rodríguez hauls himself up the Mur de Huy, ahead of Froome and a flagging Gallopin.

A stunned Tony Martin absorbs the enormity of his success, after snatching victory from some of the best sprinters in the business.

TONY MARTIN, FOURTH TIME LUCKY

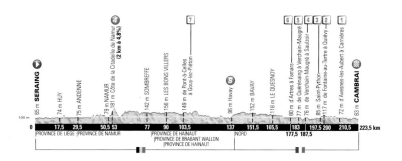

It was a very tense peloton that set out from Seraing, not only because of the memory of the previous day's terrifying crash, but also because they knew that ahead of them lay seven sectors of *pavé* totalling 13 kilometres. A notable absentee on the start line was Fabian Cancellara. The injuries sustained by Spartacus on stage three proved too serious, even for him. A CT scan revealed two cracked vertebrae, a painful reprise of the spinal fractures he suffered earlier in the season.

This was the longest stage of the 2015 Tour, at 223.5 km, and would require huge reserves of both physical and mental stamina. Unlike the previous year's cobbled stage, the rain mostly held off, so that dust, rather than mud, was the order of the day. An early breakaway was caught with 40 km and six sectors of *pavé* remaining. Then the pace increased as teams jostled for position at the front of the pack, hoping to keep out of trouble and prevent any serious moves from cobbles specialists such as Degenkolb, Van Avermaet and Sénéchal.

Nibali hit the *pavé* with gusto, clearly hoping to emulate his 2014 performance. It wasn't enough to win him the stage, but did earn him the day's award for most aggressive rider. The other favourites were more conservative. Froome, who crashed out before even reaching the cobbles in 2014, was expertly chaperoned by Geraint Thomas, whose strength as a classics rider was proved earlier in the year when he won the E3 Harelbeke.

"Next to the Worlds and the Olympics, it's really my best day on a Grand Tour."

TONY MARTIN

As the pressure piled on, the race strung out. The GC contenders managed to stay together until Thibaut Pinot suffered a puncture, followed soon after by a mechanical problem that left him raging and angrily bouncing his bike on the tarmac. His bad luck lost him over three minutes on his key rivals, scuppering the young Frenchman's chances of repeating last year's podium finish. Leaving the final *pavé* sector, and with just 10 km to go, Thomas led an attack. But the bunch eventually came back together as the teams pulled hard to position their men for the inevitable sprint finale in Cambrai. However, they hadn't reckoned on the tenacity of Tony Martin.

The previous evening, atop the Mur de Huy, Martin had looked utterly dejected, having seen Froome leapfrog him in the GC to snatch the *maillot jaune* by a single solitary second. But he hadn't given up his dream of wearing yellow. Tucked into the leading group, alongside his team mate Mark Cavendish — another man hungry for glory — Martin bided his time. Then, with just 3.4 km to go, the triple World Time Trial champion powered away as only he could, never easing up until he crossed the line, a full three seconds ahead of his pursuers. Finally, after three days of frustration, the yellow jersey was his. His compatriot John Degenkolb placed second, but had the consolation of knowing that with Greipel in green and Martin in yellow, Germany was dominating the first part of this dramatic Tour. ∎

CLASSIFICATION FOR STAGE 4

1. MARTIN Tony (GER, Etixx – Quick-Step) 5h28'58"
2. Degenkolb J (GER, Giant-Alpecin) +3"
3. Sagan P (SVK, Tinkoff-Saxo) +3"
4. Van Avermaet G (BEL, BMC) +3"
5. Boasson Hagen E (NOR, MTN-Qhubeka) +3"
6. Bouhanni N (FRA, Cofidis) +3"
7. Guarnieri J (ITA, Katusha) +3"
8. Gallopin T (FRA, Lotto-Soudal) +3"
9. Štybar Z (CZE, Etixx – Quick-Step) +3"
10. Coquard B (FRA, Europcar) +3"
11. Valverde A (ESP, Movistar) +3"
12. Cavendish M (GBR, Etixx – Quick-Step) +3".
13. Urán R (COL, Etixx – Quick-Step) +3"
14. Gesink R (NED, Lotto NL-Jumbo) +3"
15. Nibali V (ITA, Astana) +3"

Winner's average speed: 40.8 km/h
Did not start: Schillinger A (GER, Bora-Argon 18), Cancellara F (SUI, Trek), Impey D (RSA, Orica-GreenEdge)

GENERAL CLASSIFICATION

1. MARTIN Tony (GER, Etixx – Quick-Step) 12h 40'26"
2. Froome C (GBR, Sky) +12"
3. van Garderen T (USA, BMC) +25"
4. Gallopin T (FRA, Lotto-Soudal) +38"
5. Sagan P (SVK, Tinkoff-Saxo) +39"
6. Van Avermaet G (BEL, BMC) +40"
7. Urán R (COL, Etixx – Quick-Step) +46"
8. Contador A (ESP, Tinkoff-Saxo) +48"
9. Thomas G (GBR, Sky) +1'15"
10. Štybar Z (CZE, Etixx – Quick-Step) +1'16"
11. Barguil W (FRA, Giant-Alpecin) +1'19"
12. Mollema B (NED, Trek) +1'44"
13. Nibali V (ITA, Astana) +1'50"
14. Gesink R (NED, LottoNL-Jumbo) +1'51"
15. Kreuziger R (CZE, Tinkoff-Saxo) +2'03"

MARTIN T
(GER, ETIXX – QUICK-STEP)

GREIPEL A
(GER, LOTTO-SOUDAL)

RODRÍGUEZ J
(ESP, KATUSHA)

SAGAN P
(SVK, TINKOFF-SAXO)

Team classification

BMC RACING TEAM: 38h02'55"

MOST AGGRESSIVE RIDER
NIBALI V (ITA, ASTANA)

The peloton rolls smoothly over the placid waters of the Meuse, at the start in Seraing. Ahead of them lies a potentially perilous stage.

(Top) Belgian flags greet the riders as they reach the *pavé*. Yet it's a German who'll win the day.
(Bottom) Against all expectations, Froome proves to be quite at ease on the cobbles, unlike Contador behind him, who appears to be suffering.

World Road Race Champion
Michał Kwiatkowski battles
the dust and the cobbles,
in a scene worthy of
the Paris-Roubaix.

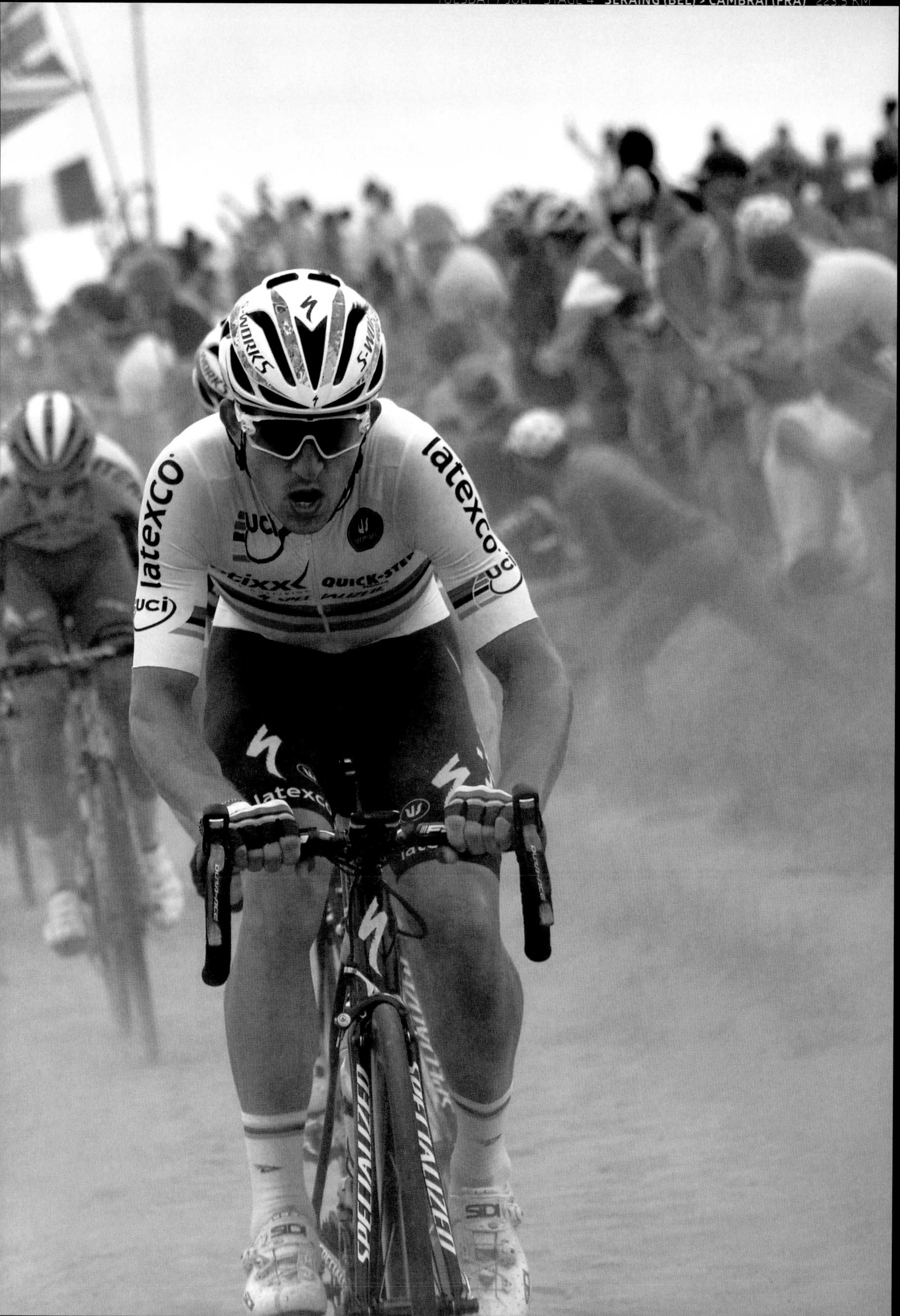

THE ART
OF AVOIDING A FALL

The cobbles made their first appearance on the Tour in 1985, on a stage from Neufchâtel-en-Bray to Roubaix, a town synonymous with the cobbled classics, chief of which is the Paris-Roubaix. But the introduction of the pavé was controversial, with opinions divided along two lines: some considered that, despite the risks, riding the cobbles was a cycling discipline in its own right; others felt that it was foolhardy to send the peloton belting down rough tracks that could blow a race leader's chances in just a few kilometres. There were indeed a number of crashes during that first stage, but most of them actually occurred on surfaced sections of the route. None of the favourites were adversely affected by this supposedly calamitous day, and the doom mongers soon quietened down.

The cobbled sections have always been relatively short: 10.5 km in 1985, 8.5 km in 1989, and only 3.4 km in 2004. However, in 2010 the third stage included a longer section of 13.5 km between Wanze and Arenberg. The terrain suited the day's winner, Thor Hushovd, but the *pavé* proved deadly for Tour favourite Fränk Schleck, who was forced to withdraw from the race. Yet it has never been the cobbles themselves as much as the rain that makes conditions treacherous. Stage five of the 2014 Tour, from Ypres to Arenberg Porte du Hainaut, is a case in point. It was there that the defending champion Christopher Froome's bid for victory came to an end. The British rider fell twice and was forced to withdraw at kilometre 83, before the peloton had even reached the first of the 13 km of cobbled sections. Just as in 2010, it was the weather that made the stage so tough, with the road surface proving to be a secondary factor. But it's not just the weather; nerves can play their part as well. The explosive mixture of cobbles, rain and the fearsome reputation of the pavé can make riders so jittery that they become the cause of their own downfall. ■

TOUR DE FRANCE 1985
To avoid pitfalls, Bernard Hinault (right) rides at the front of the peloton in his famous La Vie Claire jersey. He would reach Paris as the winner.

TOUR DE FRANCE 2014
Vincenzo Nibali masters the *pavé* and the harsh weather conditions. He would go on to win the Tour. Could the *pavé* stages be early indicators of final victory?

"I haven't crashed all year, and now, three times in ten days. That's a lot of bad luck in a period containing all my major goals." Nacer Bouhani, after withdrawing 10 km into the stage.

ANDRÉ GREIPEL STRIKES AGAIN

When questioned at the start, John Degenkolb predicted that this stage would present many similarities to day two in Zeeland. And as strong winds and rain battered the peloton, he was proved right. While stage four was expected to be much more dramatic than it actually was, the fifth stage would turn out to be highly stressful for the peloton, not so much for its impact on the GC, but for its litany of crashes and mishaps.

The route skirted the battlefields of the Great War, but the day was not about offensives, rather the preservation of existing forces. In this prudent yet risky struggle, it was Nacer Bouhanni who was the first to fall. Just 10 km into the stage he was involved in a pile-up that put an end to his Tour de France. It was a double blow for the young Cofidis sprinter, who only confirmed his participation in the Tour at the last minute, after crashing in the closing stages of the French national championships just ten days before.

Pierre-Luc Périchon, of Bretagne-Séché Environment, made an early escape and pursued a solo breakaway. He was out on in his own for 90 km, a tough place to be, but possibly preferable to the main bunch, which suffered a whole series of crashes as the race twisted and turned its way through the Somme. Bryan Coquard, Greg Van Avermaet and André Greipel were just some of the riders who went down. In retrospect, this was a clear sign of the pressure the sprinters were under.

For the last three days, Tinkoff-Saxo had been pursuing the strategy of *coup de bordure* — attempting to attack when the wind carves the peloton into echelons. Having covered 110 km, and with crosswinds strafing the main field, Tinkoff-Saxo, along with their allies of circumstance, BMC, managed to force a gap. This time though, the favourites were all on the right side of the split. But 25 km from Amiens, a slight touch of the brakes on the rain-soaked roadway was all it took to send a whole mass of riders in the leading bunch sliding to the floor, as if they had cycled onto an ice rink. Among them was the unlucky Thibaut Pinot — never can a rider have been so keen to reach the mountains.

With a mass sprint on the cards, the contending teams began to get organised. The *maillot jaune*, Tony Martin, turned zealous *domestique* and set a cracking pace for Mark Cavendish's lead-out train. Peter Sagan, John Degenkolb, Alexander Kristoff, Arnaud Démare and Bryan Coquard were also in the mix. The road was dry and conditions looked good for Cavendish, who was hugging Kristoff's wheel. But once again he launched too soon, 300 metres from the line, and despite the fiercest of sprints, he couldn't match the more patient André Greipel, who surged past and stormed to victory. ∎

> *"Win two stages and reinforce my green jersey, what more could you ask for?"*
> **ANDRÉ GREIPEL**

CLASSIFICATION FOR STAGE 5

1. GREIPEL André (GER, Lotto-Soudal) 4h39'00"
2. Sagan P (SVK, Tinkoff-Saxo) +0"
3. Cavendish M (GBR, Etixx – Quick-Step) +0"
4. Kristoff A (NOR, Katusha) +0"
5. Boasson Hagen E (NOR, MTN-Qhubeka) +0"
6. Degenkolb J (GER, Giant-Alpecin) +0"
7. Démare A (FRA, FDJ) +0"
8. Coquard B (FRA, Europcar) +0"
9. Cimolai D (ITA, Lampre-Merida) +0"
10. Van Avermaet G (BEL, BMC) +0"
11. Soupe G (FRA, Cofidis) +0"
12. Dempster Z (AUS, Bora-Argon 18) +0"
13. Janse van Rensburg R (RSA, MTN-Qhubeka) +0"
14. Pantano J (COL, IAM) +0"
15. Vanmarcke S (BEL, LottoNL-Jumbo) +0"

Winner's average speed: 40.8 km/h
Did not finish: Bouhanni N (FRA, Cofidis),
Bauer J (NZL, Cannondale-Garmin)

GENERAL CLASSIFICATION

1. MARTIN Tony (GER, Etixx – Quick-Step) 17h19'26"
2. Froome C (GBR, Sky) +12"
3. van Garderen T (USA, BMC) +25"
4. Sagan P (SVK, Tinkoff-Saxo) +33"
5. Gallopin T (FRA, Lotto-Soudal) +38"
6. Van Avermaet G (BEL, BMC) +40"
7. Urán R (COL, Etixx – Quick-Step) +46"
8. Contador A (ESP, Tinkoff-Saxo) +48"
9. Thomas G (GBR, Sky) +1'15"
10. Štybar Z (CZE, Etixx – Quick-Step) +1'16"
11. Barguil W (FRA, Giant-Alpecin) +1'19"
12. Mollema B (NED, Trek) +1'44"
13. Nibali V (ITA, Astana) +1'50"
14. Gesink R (NED, LottoNL-Jumbo) +1'51"
15. Kreuziger R (CZE, Tinkoff-Saxo) +2'03"

MARTIN T
(GER, ETIXX –QUICK-STEP)

GREIPEL A
(GER, LOTTO-SOUDAL)

RODRÍGUEZ J
(ESP, KATUSHA)

SAGAN P
(SVK, TINKOFF-SAXO)

Team classification

BMC RACING TEAM:
51h59'55"

MOST AGGRESSIVE RIDER
MATTHEWS M (AUS, ORICA-GREENEDGE)

André Greipel beats Peter Sagan and Mark Cavendish into second and third places. The 32-year-old sprinter is at the peak of his craft, dominating the sprints in the first part of the 2015 Tour de France.

Štybar crosses the line in first place. Little does he know that his team leader and *maillot jaune*, Tony Martin, has crashed 1 km back.

ŠTYBAR GRINS
AS MARTIN GRIMACES

The sun was finally out and shining brightly over the race, as the peloton headed out of Abbeville. Their destination was Le Havre, which had not seen a Tour stage finish since Mario Cipollini won there in 1995, and where, in 1991, stage winner Thierry Marie claimed the second longest Tour de France breakaway: 234 km — the longest was 253 km, a record set by Albert Bourlon in 1947. But stage nine of the 2015 edition will also go down in Tour history, thanks to the Eritrean rider Daniel Teklehaimanot, who became the first African cyclist to wear the polka dot jersey. The achievement followed his success at the 2015 Critérium du Dauphiné, where he won the mountains classification. Riding for the South African team, MTN-Qhubeka, Teklehaimanot, with his fluid, yet determined pedalling style and his attacking spirit, embodies the dawn of a new era for African cycling.

It all started with a banal breakaway, launched just 5 km from the start by the indefatigable Perrig Quéméneur of Europcar. He was joined by Teklehaimanot and by the Belgian rider Kenneth Vanbilsen of Cofidis, who threw himself into the action, having recovered from a crash the previous day. It was the trio's long breakaway that gave Teklehaimanot the opportunity to pick up the points necessary to show off the polka dot jersey on that evening's podium. For his efforts, Quéméneur was crowned the day's most aggressive rider, after notching up more than 400 km of accumulated breakaway since the start of the Tour.

But the day's true drama was concentrated in the final kilometre, where a 7% climb up to a short finishing straight saw the riders bunch up at a relatively slow 18 km/h, a recipe for disaster. Tony Martin clipped wheels with the rider in front and veered sideways into Barguil and Nibali. All three fell, taking out van Garderen and Quintana, who landed on top of them in an ungainly, yet star-studded sprawl of Tour favourites. Nudged by Nibali on his way down, Froome tottered precariously, but just managed to stay upright. As for Martin, his own tumble left him sitting on the tarmac, left arm held across his chest in the all too recognisable position of a man who has just broken his collarbone.

In a moving display of *esprit de corps*, Martin was nursed to the line by his team mates, almost certainly realising that his Tour was over. It seemed, after Cancellara's misfortune on stage three, that the curse of the *maillot jaune* had struck again. Despite the devastating blow dealt to their leader, Etixx–Quick-Step could at least savour the consolation of stage victory. Zdeněk Štybar, unaware of the drama unfolding behind him, attacked 300 metres out, taking the stage, and leaving second-placed Peter Sagan to rue yet another missed opportunity. ■

> *"This victory means as much to me as my first victory in the Cyclo-cross World Championships."*
> **ZDENĚK ŠTYBAR**

CLASSIFICATION FOR STAGE 6

1. ŠTYBAR Zdeněk (CZE, Etixx – Quick-Step), 4h53'46"
2. Sagan P (SVK, Tinkoff-Saxo) +2"
3. Coquard B (FRA, Europcar) +2"
4. Degenkolb J (GER, Giant-Alpecin) +2"
5. Van Avermaet G (BEL, BMC) +2"
6. Gallopin T (FRA, Lotto-Soudal) +2"
7. Boasson Hagen E (NOR, MTN-Qhubeka) +2"
8. Cimolai D (ITA, Lampre-Merida) +2"
9. Simon J (FRA, Cofidis) +2"
10. Izagirre G (ESP, Movistar) +2"
11. Kristoff A (NOR, Katusha) +2"
12. Gesink R (NED, LottoNL-Jumbo) +2"
13. Rodríguez J (ESP, Katusha) +2"
14. Fonseca A (FRA, Bretagne-Séché) +2"
15. Valverde A (ESP, Movistar) +2"

Winner's average speed: 39.1 km/h
Did not start: Albasini M (SUI, Orica-GreenEdge)

GENERAL CLASSIFICATION

1. MARTIN Tony (GER, Etixx – Quick-Step) 22h11'14"
2. Froome C (GBR, Sky) +12"
3. van Garderen T (USA, BMC) +25"
4. Sagan P (SVK, Tinkoff-Saxo) +27"
5. Gallopin T (FRA, Lotto-Soudal) +38"
6. Van Avermaet G (BEL, BMC) +40"
7. Urán R (COL, Etixx – Quick-Step) +46"
8. Contador A (ESP, Tinkoff-Saxo) +48"
9. Štybar Z (CZE, Etixx – Quick-Step) +1'46"
10. Thomas G (GBR, Sky) +1'15"
11. Barguil W (FRA, Giant-Alpecin) +1'19"
12. Mollema B (NED, Trek) +1'44"
13. Nibali V (ITA, Astana) +1'50"
14. Gesink R (NED, LottoNL-Jumbo) +1'51"
15. Kreuziger R (CZE, Tinkoff-Saxo) +2'03"

MARTIN T
(GER, ETIXX – QUICK-STEP)

GREIPEL A
(GER, LOTTO-SOUDAL)

TEKLEHAIMANOT D
(ERI, MTN-QHUBEKA)

SAGAN P
(SVK, TINKOFF-SAXO)

Team classification

BMC RACING TEAM:
66h41'19"

MOST AGGRESSIVE RIDER
QUÉMÉNEUR P (FRA, EUROPCAR)

The two survivors of the morning's breakaway, Kenneth Vanbilsen (Cofidis) and Perrig Quéméneur (Europcar) refuse to accept defeat. At 15 km from the finish, the Belgian would go it alone, before being caught 3 km from the line.

(Top) Just a few hundred metres from the finish, Tony Martin nurses a broken collarbone, his hopes of continued Tour success in tatters.

(Bottom) The *maillot jaune* is escorted to the line by his team mates, including the World Champion, Michał Kwiatkowski. Twice in three days, the wearer of the yellow jersey has been forced to withdraw following a crash. Glory demands a high price.

The Eritrean Daniel Teklehaimanot, the first African to wear the polka dot jersey, poses for a historic photo.

A triumphant Mark Cavendish celebrates his twenty-sixth Tour de France stage win, and his first in any Grand Tour since 2013.

CAVENDISH MAKES HIS MARK

S tage seven would start without the *maillot jaune*, indeed without any *maillot jaune*. Despite his injuries, Tony Martin crossed the line and retained yellow in Le Havre, but abandoned overnight, leaving the tour without a leader. Nevertheless, with neither cobbles nor crosswinds, and just the fourth-category Côte de Canapville 12 km from the start — where the polka dot jersey contenders would be keen to pick up points — this looked like being a relatively calm stage after a stressful first week. There was one minor drama in the neutralised zone — Alberto Contador and Robert Gesink were caught up in a crash, apparently while chatting about ... crashes. Both riders escaped unscathed, and the peloton pedalled out of Livarot, heading from Normandy to Brittany, two provinces that have produced many a Tour de France star over the years. But the real show was scheduled for Fougères, where the sprinters would have their last chance to shine before the race hit the Pyrenees. The cast was drawn from the finest performers on the circuit: all or nothing André Greipel, in the green jersey; Peter Sagan, wearing white, but wanting more; and Mark Cavendish, desperate to prove that he is the fastest man on two wheels. Add Degenkolb and Kristoff, and it was all set for an explosive finale.

At 1.5 km into the stage, five men broke away: Kristijan Durasek, Daniel Teklehaimanot, Luis Ángel Maté, Brice Feillu and Anthony Delaplace. The last two were particularly keen to show their mettle, since not only was their team, Bretagne-Séché, riding into home territory, but Delaplace hails from Normandy, where the stage began. Teklehaimanot's motivation was claiming the single mountains point on offer, to consolidate his lead in the polka dot jersey competition. 32 km from the finish, Maté attacked, but the Eritrean opted not chase, his job done for the day. With 10 km to go, the peloton had caught all the breakaway riders, and a sprint finish was in the offing.

All the big guns were there, elbow to elbow. But unlike stages two and five, when Cavendish went too early, this time it was Greipel who pounced too soon. Delivered neatly onto Kristoff's wheel by Mark Renshaw, Cavendish calmly waited until Greipel pulled past him with 300 metres to go. Then the Manx Missile launched himself, head down, out of the saddle, in his trademark style. For a moment, it looked like he might be boxed in, but he found a gap and ducked through, beating Greipel to the line. Sagan took third by barely half a wheel.

It had been a roller-coaster week for Ettix – Quick-Step, but in Fougères they truly showed their class. This was a much-needed win for the team, and for Cav, who dedicated the victory to his absent teammate, Tony Martin. On the podium, Chris Froome again donned yellow, capping a great day out for the Brits. ∎

"I had the same power the other days, but it was a question of timing to make it a victory this time."

MARK CAVENDISH

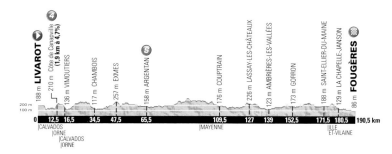

CLASSIFICATION FOR STAGE 7

1. CAVENDISH Mark (GBR, Etixx – Quick-Step) 4h27'25"
2. Greipel A (GER, Lotto-Soudal) +0"
3. Sagan P (SVK, Tinkoff-Saxo) +0"
4. Degenkolb J (GER, Giant-Alpecin) +0"
5. Kristoff A (NOR, Katusha) +0"
6. Démare A (FRA, FDJ) +0"
7. Farrar T (USA, MTN-Qhubeka) +0"
8. Janse van Rensburg R (RSA, MTN-Qhubeka) +0"
9. Cimolai D (ITA, Lampre-Merida) +0"
10. Bennett S (IRL, Bora-Argon 18) +0"
11. Navardauskas R (LTU, Cannondale-Garmin) +0"
12. Coquard B (FRA, Europcar) +0"
13. Vachon F (FRA, Bretagne-Séché) +0"
14. Guarnieri J (ITA, Katusha) +0"
15. Soupe G (FRA, Cofidis) +0"

Winner's average speed: 42.7 km/h
Did not start: Martin T (GER, Etixx – Quick-Step), Henderson G (NZL, Lotto-Soudal)

GENERAL CLASSIFICATION

1. FROOME Christopher (GBR, Sky) 26h40'51"
2. Sagan P (SVK, Tinkoff-Saxo) +11"
3. van Garderen T (USA, BMC) +13"
4. Gallopin T (FRA, Lotto-Soudal) +26"
5. Van Avermaet G (BEL, BMC) +28"
6. Urán R (COL, Etixx – Quick-Step) +34"
7. Contador A (ESP, Tinkoff-Saxo) +36"
8. Štybar Z (CZE, Etixx – Quick-Step) +52"
9. Thomas G (GBR, Sky) +1'03"
10. Barguil W (FRA, Giant-Alpecin) +1'07"
11. Mollema B (NED, Trek) +1'32"
12. Nibali V (ITA, Astana) +1'38"
13. Gesink R (NED, LottoNL-Jumbo) +1'39"
14. Kreuziger R (CZE, Tinkoff-Saxo) +1'51"
15. Valverde A (ESP, Movistar) +1'51"

FROOME C
(GBR, SKY)

GREIPEL A
(GER, LOTTO-SOUDAL)

TEKLEHAIMANOT D
(ERI, MTN-QHUBEKA)

SAGAN P
(SVK, TINKOFF-SAXO)

Team classification

BMC RACING TEAM:
80h03'34"

MOST AGGRESSIVE RIDER
DELAPLACE A (FRA, BRETAGNE-SÉCHÉ)

Brice Feillu and Anthony Delaplace take their turns on the front of a long breakaway. Their Brittany-based team, Bretagne-Séché, had focussed on this stage, which finished on home territory in Fougères.

THE HEART OF FRENCH CYCLING

B rittany has long been a key region for French cycling. It first welcomed the Tour on 27 July 1905, when the ninth stage, starting in La Rochelle, finished in Rennes. French rider Louis Trousselier won the day, and went on to win the Tour.

At a time when *La Grande Boucle* visited every major part of France, Brittany was a first class destination. But it was not until 1927 that a Breton achieved success on home ground: Ferdinand Le Drogo, from Pontivy, riding for the Dilecta-Wolber team, carried off the 199 kilometre fifth stage from Cherbourg to Dinan. Two years later, it was Ferdinand's brother, Paul Le Drogo, riding for the same team, who won the sixth stage from the Breton town of Vannes to Les Sables-d'Olonne.

In 1953 and 1954, Paul Le Drogo was *directeur sportif* for the Stella-Wolber team, which included a rosy-cheeked Breton from Saint-Méen-le-Grand in Ille-et-Vilaine by the name of Louison Bobet. Bobet won the Tour both of those years, and then again in 1955, becoming the first rider to win three consecutive editions of the Tour de France.

But Bobet wasn't the first Breton Tour winner. He was a worthy successor to the valiant Jean Robic, who claimed the first post-war edition of the Tour in 1947. Born in the Ardennes to parents originally from Morbihan, he was nicknamed "Biquet" (kid goat), as well as "Tête de cuir" (leather head) owing to his habit of always wearing a leather crash helmet. Robic was bad-tempered, provocative and a daredevil, his rustic demeanour in sharp contrast to that of his elegant, image-conscious rival, Louison Bobet. Riding for Équipe de l'Ouest (managed by Pierre Cloare, winner of two Tour stages in 1939) Robic won the Tour in 1947, only claiming the *maillot jaune* on the final stage — something that had never happened before. He managed to rack up six more stage wins by 1953, the year he also succeeded in wearing the yellow jersey for a day, the only time in his career, winning it on Bastille Day on the mountain stage to Luchon.

Robic patented the tradition of the tenacious, bellicose Breton cyclist we would later recognise in Bernard Hinault, five-times winner of the Tour de France (1978, 1979, 1981, 1982 and 1985), a record equalled only by Jacques Anquetil, Eddy Merckx and Miguel Indurain.

Having welcomed the Tour so many times and produced such great champions, Brittany will always hold a special place in the heart of French cycling. ∎

> *Having welcomed the Tour so many times and produced such great champions, Brittany will always hold a special place in the heart of French cycling.*

Alexis Vuillermoz savours
his first major victory
in professional cycling,
on the Mûr-de-Bretagne.
He is that rarest of riders,
a combination of climber
and *puncheur*.

ALEXIS VUILLERMOZ, KING OF THE MÛR

For the second time in the 2015 Tour, the race would finish on a mur: the Mûr de Bretagne. Longer than stage three's Mur de Huy, with an average gradient of 7%, and dead straight for its first 1.5 km — after 180 km of riding, there would be nowhere to hide. There also was nowhere for the Italian rider Luca Paolini to hide. The Katusha rider tested positive for cocaine following an anti-doping control after stage four, and was promptly withdrawn from the race by his team.

This hilly stage served to remind the riders that the tough gradients of the Pyrenees were not far off. Among the hills, there was potential for changes in the classifications. The Slovak rider, Peter Sagan, was already wearing white, but had his sights firmly set on dislodging André Greipel to take green, as well as swiping yellow from Chris Froome, just eleven seconds ahead. Carried by their speed through the intermediate sprint – won by Greipel – a group broke away from the main field, containing, among others, Sagan, Greipel, Cavendish and world champion Michał Kwiatkowski. With so many top sprinters in the group, the GC teams were never going to let them get away, and with 8 km remaining, the last of the breakaway riders were caught.

The main battle played out in the final two kilometres, when the front of the peloton, with all the main protagonists, arrived at the foot of the Mûr. Leading them was Team Sky, seemingly poised to launch Froome, who made a fierce acceleration that Vincenzo Nibali couldn't follow. Contador settled into Froome's wheel, as did Quintana, though whether they were tired or merely keeping their cards close to their chests, it was impossible to tell. Also near the front of the field was the frisky Warren Barguil, a revelation of the Tour, as well as Tony Gallopin, showing striking maturity to stay in complete control of his own race, whatever the circumstances. And though Thibaut Pinot and Romain Bardet appeared to be struggling, the same could not be said for the climber from AG2R La Mondiale, Alexis Vuillermoz — 800 metres from the finish, he attacked. Irishman Dan Martin chased valiantly, but Vuillermoz was too distant and too determined, punching for the line with panache. Riding in his second Tour, the twenty-seven year old from Saint-Claude, in the Jura, served up France's first victory in this year's race.

As for Sagan, he didn't manage to take yellow, but the green jersey was his. The Slovakian crossed the finish line fourth, earning the points he needed. Quite something for a man yet to win a single stage.

All the main favourites finished together, apart from Nibali, trailing his opponents by ten seconds and dropping to thirteenth place, at 1'48". If the diminutive Mûr de Bretagne could crack Nibali, what would the Pyrenees do to him? ∎

"I'd had the Huy stage marked out in advance, and I came third. The Mûr stage I won. I've not missed any of my goals."

ALEXIS VUILLERMOZ

CLASSIFICATION FOR STAGE 8

1. VUILLERMOZ Alexis (FRA, AG2R) 4h20'55"
2. Martin D (IRL, Cannondale-Garmin) +5"
3. Valverde A (ESP, Movistar) +10"
4. Sagan P (SVK, Tinkoff-Saxo) +10"
5. Gallopin T (FRA, Lotto-Soudal) +10"
6. Van Avermaet G (BEL, BMC) +10"
7. Yates A (GBR, Orica-GreenEdge) +10"
8. Froome C (GBR, Sky) +10"
9. Mollema B (NED, Trek) +10"
10. van Garderen T (USA, BMC) +10"
11. Arredondo J (COL, Trek) +10"
12. Rodríguez J (ESP, Katusha) +10"
13. Barguil W (FRA, Giant-Alpecin) +10"
14. Contador A (ESP, Tinkoff-Saxo) +10"
15. Urán R (COL, Etixx – Quick-Step) +10"

Winner's average speed: 41.7 km/h
Did not start: Paolini L (ITA, Katusha)

GENERAL CLASSIFICATION

1. FROOME Christopher (GBR, Sky) 31h01'56"
2. Sagan P (SVK, Tinkoff-Saxo) +11"
3. van Garderen T (USA, BMC) +13"
4. Gallopin T (FRA, Lotto-Soudal) +26"
5. Van Avermaet G (BEL, BMC) +28"
6. Urán R (COL, Etixx – Quick-Step) +34"
7. Contador A (ESP, Tinkoff-Saxo) +36"
8. Barguil W (FRA, Giant-Alpecin) +1'07"
9. Štybar Z (CZE, Etixx – Quick-Step) +1'15"
10. Mollema B (NED, Trek) +1'32"
11. Gesink R (NED, LottoNL-Jumbo) +1'39"
12. Valverde A (ESP, Movistar) +1'47"
13. Nibali V (ITA, Astana) +1'48"
14. Kreuziger R (CZE, Tinkoff-Saxo) +1'51"
15. Thomas G (GBR, Sky) +1'52"

FROOME C
(GBR, SKY)

SAGAN P
(SVK, TINKOFF-SAXO)

TEKLEHAIMANOT D
(ERI, MTN-QHUBEKA)

SAGAN P (SVK, TINKOFF-SAXO)
worn by Barguil W (FRA, Giant-Alpecin)

Team classification

BMC RACING TEAM:
93h06'49"

MOST AGGRESSIVE RIDER
HUZARSKI B (POL, BORA-ARGON 18)

The *maillot jaune* Chris Froome seems as surprised as anyone at Vuillermoz's attack, 800 metres from the line. This feat of bravura by the man from the Jura would pay off handsomely.

At the finish, the BMC riders celebrate their tightly contested victory.

BMC RACING, POETRY IN MOTION

Coming so late in the race, the impact of this team time trial would be unpredictable. After nine stages of racing, the riders were fatigued and many carried injuries. Not only that, but several teams had less than their full complement of riders, a handicap in an event where the finish time of the fifth-placed man is the one that counts.

At twenty-eight kilometres, the course wasn't especially long, but its three distinct sections would make it a challenge. The first, a relatively flat section, ran through a built-up area and required careful manoeuvring; the second was hillier, and with a westerly crosswind to make it all the more perilous; the third section was the shortest, but comprised the killer climb of the Côte de Cadoudal up to the finish. This being Brittany, the entire route was thronged with enthusiastic spectators.

Orica-GreenEdge, who usually excel in this discipline, were down to six men, while Etixx – Quick-Step would miss the talent of time trial specialist Tony Martin. On the other hand, the five teams with most at stake in the GC — Astana, Tinkoff-Saxo, Movistar, Sky and BMC — had all their riders on the start ramp. Of those, the reigning team time trial world champions, BMC, were arguably the strongest, and had the added motivation of potentially riding Tejay van Garderen into yellow.

The first of the favourites to roll off the start ramp were Astana. They started well, but fragmented soon after the first time check; it wasn't a convincing performance. Movistar were next. They looked good, but faltered on the climbs. Nevertheless they finished well, beating Astana by 31" and propelling Quintana past Nibali in the GC. The Colombian also claimed the white jersey from Warren Barguil. Tinkoff-Saxo finished without drama, beating Astana by 7", but trailing Movistar by 18".

If this discipline can be considered an indication of each team's cohesion and *esprit de corps*, then BMC and Sky were in good shape. Both looked well drilled as they tackled the technical *parcours*. The American team posted the best time at the first checkpoint, until the British squad equalled it minutes later. Froome spent plenty of time up front setting the pace for team Sky, piling on the pressure at each turn, and maybe that was what cracked fifth man Nicolas Roche on the final climb. The split probably cost Sky the stage, as they finished 1" down on a triumphant BMC.

It was striking how close the battle was. With the exception of Orica-GreenEdge and Cofidis, all the teams finished inside two minutes. Froome retained his yellow jersey, and put further time into his rivals, all except for van Garderen. The American may have missed out on the *maillot jaune*, but as the mountains approach, he must surely have been thinking about the podium. ■

> *"It's an incredible feeling. So far the team in the first week has been incredible. We've passed every test with flying colours."*
>
> **TEJAY VAN GARDEREN**

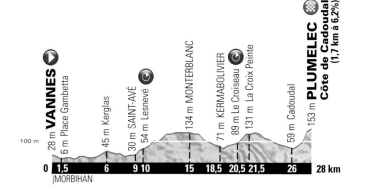

CLASSIFICATION FOR STAGE 9

1. BMC RACING TEAM (USA) 32'15"
2. Team Sky (GBR) +1"
3. Movistar Team (ESP) +4"
4. Tinkoff-Saxo (RUS) +28"
5. Astana Pro Team (KAZ) +35"
6. IAM Cycling (SUI) +38"
7. Etixx – Quick-Step (BEL) +45"
8. Lampre-Merida (ITA) +48"
9. Team LottoNL-Jumbo (NED) +1'14"
10. AG2R La Mondiale (FRA) +1'24"
11. Trek Factory Racing (USA) +1'25"
12. Team Cannondale-Garmin (USA) +1'29"
13. Bora-Argon 18 (GER) +1'32"
14. FDJ (FRA) +1'33"
15. Lotto-Soudal (BEL) +1'36"

GENERAL CLASSIFICATION

1. FROOME Christopher (GBR, Sky) 31h34'12"
2. van Garderen T (USA, BMC) +12"
3. Van Avermaet G (BEL, BMC) +27"
4. Sagan P (SVK, Tinkoff-Saxo) +38"
5. Contador A (ESP, Tinkoff-Saxo) +1'03"
6. Urán R (COL, Etixx – Quick-Step) +1'18"
7. Valverde A (ESP, Movistar) +1'50"
8. Thomas G (GBR, Sky) +1'52"
9. Quintana N (COL, Movistar) +1'59"
10. Štybar Z (CZE, Etixx – Quick-Step) +1'59"
11. Gallopin T (FRA, Lotto-Soudal) +2'01"
12. Kreuziger R (CZE Tinkoff-Saxo) +2'18"
13. Nibali V (ITA, Astana) +2'22"
14. Barguil W (FRA, Giant-Alpecin) +2'43"
15. Gesink R (NED, LottoNL-Jumbo) +2'52"

Winning team's average speed: 52.1 km/h

FROOME C
(GBR, SKY)

SAGAN P
(SVK, TINKOFF-SAXO)

TEKLEHAIMANOT D
(ERI, MTN-QHUBEKA)

SAGAN P (SVK, TINKOFF-SAXO)
worn by Quintana N (COL, Movistar)

Team classification

BMC RACING TEAM:
95h48'04"

A tidy paceline,
but Cofidis
nevertheless
finished 2'32" down.

(Top) A well-drilled
Sky misses victory
by just one second.
(Bottom) Trek are
flanked by a Breton
crowd whose enthusiasm
for cycling in general
and the Tour in particular
is as strong as ever.

Chris Froome, a man not generally known for his effusiveness, explodes with joy as he crosses the finish line first in La Pierre-Saint-Martin.

CHRIS FROOME STORMS THE PYRENEES

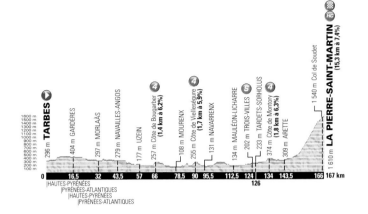

Despite a rest day in Pau, the transition to the mountains was tough for the riders, some of whom seemed to have grown accustomed to the big ring. For them, the required shift to the inner ring would be psychological as well as physical. The first Pyrenean stage of the 2015 Tour would see a summit finish at La Pierre-Saint-Martin, after an arduous 15.3 km hors-catégorie climb with an average gradient of 7.4% and ramps up to 10%.

It was Bastille Day, and accordingly a Frenchman went on the attack: Pierrick Fédrigo of Bretagne-Séché Environnement escaped in the early kilometres. He was later joined by Kenneth Vanbilsen of Cofidis, and the two leapfrogged each other ahead of the peloton, hoovering up sprint and mountain points as they went — although André Greipel managed to snatch back the green jersey from Sagan at the intermediate sprint. There was a scare when Warren Barguil crashed heavily in the feed zone, but he valiantly remounted and soldiered on, nursing cuts and bruises.

As the race hit the ascent to La Pierre-Saint-Martin, the breakaway faded, as did many other riders: Daniel Teklehaimanot, Michał Kwiatkowski and Dan Martin were among the early casualties, soon joined by Romain Bardet, Thibaut Pinot and Jean-Christophe Péraud. With 11 km to go, Gesink attacked, and the subsequent acceleration in the lead group shed even more riders, including Nibali. The sun beat down mercilessly as a savage pace was set first by Movistar and then by Sky. Realising that Contador was struggling, Geraint Thomas and Richie Porte upped the tempo. But while the Tinkoff-Saxo leader was able to limit the damage, last year's Tour winner slipped further back. Meanwhile, a game of bluff was playing out at the front, as Valverde repeatedly tried to unhitch Froome, while his team leader, Quintana, clung on in defensive mode.

Suddenly, as if deciding he'd simply had enough of his opponents' caprices, the *maillot jaune* attacked 6 km from the summit. As he flew up the road in his distinctive style, it was, as usual, impossible to tell from his contorted body and grimaces whether he was on the verge of exploding or imploding. Crossing the line solo, a beaming Froome raised his arms in celebration, the most expressive we've seen him in one and a half weeks. Behind him, Richie Porte chased down Quintana for second place — a move intended to deny the Colombian his six-second bonus.

As for the French, national honour was salvaged by Pierre Rolland and Tony Gallopin, who finished in the top ten, and Warren Barguil, who, despite his injuries, placed fifteenth, and climbed up to ninth in the GC. The day's big story, however, was how much time the main contenders had lost to Froome — and this was just the first day in the mountains. ∎

> *"It's the dream scenario, but the race is far from over."*
> **CHRISTOPHER FROOME**

CLASSIFICATION FOR STAGE 10

1. FROOME Christopher (GBR, Sky) 4h22'07"
2. Porte R (AUS, Sky) +59"
3. Quintana N (COL, Movistar) +1'04"
4. Gesink R (NED, LottoNL-Jumbo) +1'33"
5. Valverde A (ESP, Movistar) +2'01"
6. Thomas G (GBR, Sky) +2'01"
7. Yates A (GBR, Orica-GreenEdge) +2'04"
8. Rolland P (FRA, Europcar) +2'04"
9. Gallopin T (FRA, Lotto-Soudal) +2'22"
10. van Garderen T (USA, BMC) +2'30"
11. Contador A (ESP, Tinkoff-Saxo) +2'51"
12. Valls R (ESP, Lampre-Merida) +3'09"
13. Fuglsang J (DEN, Astana) +3'09"
14. Pauwels S (BEL, MTN-Qhubeka) +3'19"
15. Barguil W (FRA, Giant-Alpecin) +3'19"

Winner's average speed: 38,2 km/h
Did not start: Basso I (ITA, Tinkoff-Saxo), Boom L (NED, Astana)

GENERAL CLASSIFICATION

1. FROOME Christopher (GBR, Sky) 35h56'09"
2. van Garderen T (USA, BMC) +2'52"
3. Quintana N (COL, Movistar) +3'09"
4. Valverde A (ESP, Movistar) +4'01"
5. Thomas G (GBR, Sky) +4'03"
6. Contador A (ESP, Tinkoff-Saxo) +4'04"
7. Gallopin T (FRA, Lotto-Soudal) +4'33"
8. Gesink R (NED, LottoNL-Jumbo) +4'35"
9. Barguil W (FRA, Giant-Alpecin) +6'12"
10. Nibali V (ITA, Astana) +6'57"
11. Mollema B (NED, Trek) +7'15"
12. Urán R (COL, Etixx – Quick-Step) +7'22"
13. Fuglsang J (DEN, Astana) +8'41"
14. Péraud J-C (FRA, AG2R La Mondiale) +9'18"
15. Frank M (SUI, IAM) +9'26"

FROOME C
(GBR, SKY)

GREIPEL A
(GER, LOTTO-SOUDAL)

FROOME C (GBR, SKY)
worn by Porte R (AUS, Sky)

QUINTANA N
(COL, MOVISTAR)

Team classification

TEAM SKY:
109h04'55"

MOST AGGRESSIVE RIDER
VANBILSEN K (BEL, COFIDIS)

(Top) Chris Froome prepares
to attack van Garderen
and Valverde.
(Bottom) Smiling, or maybe
grimacing, Warren Barguil
was one of the day's heroes.

Richie Porte sprints away from Nairo Quintana to claim second place and a valuable time bonus.

Rafał Majka produced a brilliant show on the Tourmalet and the ascent to Cauterets, in the purest tradition of great climbers who relish long solo breakaways.

RAFAŁ MAJKA, A VIRTUOSO PERFORMANCE

The fearsome duo of the Aspin and the Tourmalet might usually be relied upon to shake up the GC in some way, but after the day's trek through the Pyrenees, not much had changed at the top table. However, the Tour de France is a process of slow elimination, and inevitably the heat and the gradient took their toll. Romain Bardet suffered in the truest sense, vomiting due to sunstroke on the ascent of the Tourmalet, but refusing to give in. Six other riders abandoned the race, including former world champion Rui Costa.

Throughout the day, the bunch containing Froome's main rivals was muzzled by the might of his Sky team, and was unable to launch any convincing attacks. In fact, a fast and furious peloton seemed reluctant to let anyone get away. At the intermediate sprint, eternal second-place man Peter Sagan assumed his usual position; but with Greipel only managing ninth place, the points difference was enough to give Sagan the green jersey. More attacks followed, but all were neutralised, until at 75 km a group finally managed to escape, including Rafał Majka and the indestructible Thomas Voeckler.

The breakaway group hit the Tourmalet together, before Majka broke free 7 km from the summit. He crested solo and began the descent, with Dan Martin in hot pursuit, followed by an elite group containing all of the GC favourites. The descent gave riders who lost contact on the way up a chance to catch the chasing group, an opportunity grasped by Warren Barguil, still nursing injuries from the previous day's crash. As if high-speed descending wasn't perilous enough, at one point, Barguil was forced to swerve round a herd of white Pyrenean cows crossing the road. His efforts paid off, however, and he maintained his ninth place in the GC.

On the final climb to Cauterets, despite the relatively gentle gradient, Nibali slipped off the back and out of the top ten in the GC, without ever really being able to put the other favourites to the test. Contador, too, had not shown any of his customary bravura, but did manage to remain at the front with Quintana and Valverde, and avoid losing any further time.

But the day belonged to Rafał Majka. Just as in 2014, when he won two stages and the mountains classification, his superlative climbing abilities, and capacity for riding through the pain, were once again rewarded. Riding solo to victory, the Tinkoff-Saxo climber gave his team a much needed morale boost. With the withdrawal of Ivan Basso after stage nine, following a diagnosis of testicular cancer, and in light of Contador's seeming inability to challenge Froome, it was desperately needed. Second over the line in Cauterets was Irishman Dan Martin, named most aggressive rider for the fighting spirit he showed all day, and his valiant attempt to catch Majka on the final climb. ■

> *"This victory is for my teammates, for Ivan Basso and Daniele Bennati."*
> **RAFAŁ MAJKA**

CLASSIFICATION FOR STAGE 11

1. MAJKA Rafał (POL, Tinkoff-Saxo) 5h02'01"
2. Martin D (IRL, Cannondale-Garmin) +1'
3. Buchmann E (GER, Bora-Argon 18) +1'23"
4. Pauwels S (BEL, MTN-Qhubeka) +2'08"
5. Voeckler T (FRA, Europcar) +3'34"
6. Simon J (FRA, Cofidis) +3'34"
7. Mollema B (NED, Trek) +5'11"
8. Valverde A (ESP, Movistar) +5'19"
9. Froome C (GBR, Sky) +5'21"
10. Contador A (ESP, Tinkoff-Saxo) +5'21"
11. Quintana N (COL, Movistar) +5'21"
12. Sánchez S (ESP, BMC) +5'21"
13. van Garderen T (USA, BMC) +5'21"
14. Thomas G (GBR, Sky) +5'21"
15. Gesink R (NED, LottoNL-Jumbo) +5'21"

Winner's average speed: 37.3 km/h

Did not finish: Nerz D (GER, Bora-Argon 18), Costa R (POR, Lampre-Merida), Bennati D (ITA, Tinkoff-Saxo), Vansummeren J (BEL, AG2R La Mondiale), Gastauer B (LUX, AG2R La Mondiale), Taaramäe R (EST, Astana)

GENERAL CLASSIFICATION

1. FROOME Christopher (GBR, Sky) 41h03'31"
2. van Garderen T (USA, BMC) +2'52"
3. Quintana N (COL, Movistar) +3'09"
4. Valverde A (ESP, Movistar) +3'59"
5. Thomas G (GBR, Sky) +4'03"
6. Contador A (ESP, Tinkoff-Saxo) +4'04"
7. Gallopin T (FRA, Lotto-Soudal) +4'33"
8. Gesink R (NED, LottoNL-Jumbo) +4'35"
9. Barguil W (FRA, Giant-Alpecin) +6'44"
10. Mollema B (NED, Trek) +7'05"
11. Nibali V (ITA, Astana) +7'47"
12. Frank M (SUI, IAM) +9'26"
13. Sánchez S (ESP, BMC) +10'27"
14. Rolland P (FRA, Europcar) +13'57"
15. Talansky A (USA, Cannondale-Garmin) +16'33"

FROOME C (GBR, SKY)

SAGAN P (SVK, TINKOFF-SAXO)

FROOME C (GBR, SKY) worn by Porte R (AUS, Sky)

QUINTANA N (COL, MOVISTAR)

Team classification

TEAM SKY: 124h30'54"

MOST AGGRESSIVE RIDER MARTIN D (IRL, CANNONDALE-GARMIN)

The Tours pass, and Thomas Voeckler remains the same. As audacious as ever, he possesses an innate sense of race tactics.

(Top) The imperious Sky team protect their leader in all circumstances. (Bottom) Emanuel Buchmann descends in front of the valiant Dan Martin. With his compatriots Greipel and Degenkolb some way behind on this mountain stage, the German relished some time in the limelight.

After a difficult first week,
Pierre Rolland leads the peloton
up the Tourmalet.

Joaquim "Purito" Rodríguez grits his teeth as he rides solo to the summit of the Plateau de Beille, winning his second stage of the 2015 Tour.

JOAQUIM RODRÍGUEZ, RIDER ON THE STORM

Intent on creating as much drama as possible, the organisers of this year's Tour planned a mountain-packed third Pyrenean stage: four climbs, each more difficult than the last, climaxing with the *pièce de resistance*, the *hors catégorie* Plateau de Beille, described by race director Christian Prudhomme as "the Alpe d'Huez plus two kilometres". And as if that weren't enough, the race started under a baking sun, and ended in a maelstrom of thunder, lightning, rain and hailstones.

The first challenge *en route* wasn't a mountain — Lotto-Soudal took control straight away to put their man, André Greipel, in position for the intermediate sprint at 20 km. He duly won, but Sagan snatched third and maintained his position in the green jersey standings. Almost immediately after the sprint, a breakaway group of twenty-two was established, among them Joaquim Rodríguez, victor of stage three on the Mur de Huy, as well as Jakob Fuglsang, a fully resurrected Romain Bardet, and world champion, Michał Kwiatkowski.

The group built up a six minute lead as they climbed the Col de Portet d'Aspet, passing the memorial to the Italian rider, Fabio Casartelli, who died after crashing there during stage fifteen of the 1995 Tour. Twenty years have passed, but the peloton still remembers.

Kwiatkowski, joined by Sep Vanmarcke and Georg Preidler, escaped the breakaway after the descent of the Col de la Core. They gained time over the Port de Lers, but lost Preidler, who was soon passed by a chase group including Rodríguez, Bardet and Fuglsang. Meanwhile, behind, the yellow jersey group, led by Sky, tapped out a steady rhythm.

As the race hit the steep gradient of the Plateau de Beille, storms swept the road, and the race intensified. Rodríguez attacked, taking Bardet and Fuglsang with him. Ahead, Kwiatkowski was now riding with his sights set on glory, but it wasn't to be. With 8 km to go, Rodríguez dropped first Bardet, then Fuglsang, before catching and passing Kwiatkowski. Further down the mountain, Froome's challengers knew it was time make their moves if they were ever going to put the yellow jersey under pressure.

Contador was first to attack, but it was never really convincing. Implacable, the Sky train barely twitched, continuing to pound out the pace, and Contador was soon back in the bunch. Next it was Nibali's turn, then Valverde, then Quintana. One after another they made their moves, but all to no avail. At one point, the *maillot jaune* himself made a vicious little sortie that cooled his opponents' ardour — but almost cooked Geraint Thomas in the process. Perhaps dampened by the heavy rain, the big guns failed to fire. Rodríguez, on the other hand, kept his powder dry, and rode solo to his second stage victory in this year's Tour de France. ∎

> *"I'm like Atlético Madrid – you never really know what to expect from me."*
> **JOAQUIM RODRÍGUEZ**

CLASSIFICATION FOR STAGE 12

1. RODRÍGUEZ Joaquim (ESP, Katusha) 5h40'14"
2. Fuglsang J (DEN, Astana) +1'12"
3. Bardet R (FRA, AG2R La Mondiale) +1'49"
4. Izagirre G (ESP, Movistar) +4'34"
5. Meintjes L (RSA, MTN-Qhubeka) +4'38"
6. Barta J (CZE, Bora-Argon 18) +5'47"
7. Sicard R (FRA, Europcar) +6'03"
8. Chérel M (FRA, AG2R La Mondiale) +6'28"
9. Valverde A (ESP, Movistar) +6'46"
10. Froome C (GBR, Sky) +6'47"
11. Quintana N (COL, Movistar) +6'47"
12. Pinot T (FRA, FDJ) +6'47"
13. van Garderen T (USA, BMC) +6'47"
14. Contador A (ESP, Tinkoff-Saxo) +6'47"
15. Rolland P (FRA, Europcar) +6'47"

Winner's average speed: 34.4 km/h
Did not finish: Dempster Z (AUS, Bora-Argon 18), Dowsett A (GBR, Movistar)

GENERAL CLASSIFICATION

1. FROOME Christopher (GBR, Sky) 46h50'32"
2. van Garderen T (USA, BMC) +2'52"
3. Quintana N (COL, Movistar) +3'09"
4. Valverde A (ESP, Movistar) +3'58"
5. Thomas G (GBR, Sky) +4'03"
6. Contador A (ESP, Tinkoff-Saxo) +4'04"
7. Gesink R (NED, LottoNL-Jumbo) +5'32"
8. Gallopin T (FRA, Lotto-Soudal) +7'32"
9. Nibali V (ITA, Astana) +7'47"
10. Mollema B (NED, Trek) +8'02"
11. Barguil W (FRA, Giant-Alpecin) +9'43"
12. Frank M (SUI, IAM) +12'25"
13. Sánchez S (ESP, BMC) +12'53"
14. Fuglsang J (DEN, Astana) +13'33"
15. Rodríguez J (ESP, Katusha) +13'45"

FROOME C (GBR, SKY)

SAGAN P (SVK, TINKOFF-SAXO)

FROOME C (GBR, SKY)
worn by Rodríguez J (ESP, Katusha)

QUINTANA N (COL, MOVISTAR)

Team classification

MOVISTAR TEAM:
141h52'29"

MOST AGGRESSIVE RIDER
KWIATKOWSKI M (POL, ETIXX – QUICK-STEP)

(Top) Halfway through the Tour, Tony Gallopin was the best-placed Frenchman in the GC, thanks to his determination and racing savvy.
(Bottom) Their build may be better suited to racing classics, but Kwiatkowski (named the day's most aggressive rider) and Vanmarcke still dream of victory on the Plateau de Beille.

A beautiful day for Romain Bardet, who rode with courage to claim a well-deserved third place.

8 km from the finish, Nibali takes the lead, and for a few hundred precious metres the 2014 Tour champion re-emerges.

(Top) Geraint Thomas, who has proved to be a lynchpin of his Sky team, leads the *maillot jaune* through the pouring rain.
(Bottom) Nairo Quintana, the man from the Colombian high plains, tries his luck, despite knowing that Froome and Thomas will almost certainly reel him back.

A SIGN OF FUTURE POTENTIAL

The white jersey was introduced in 1975 to distinguish the best young rider in the general classification. A "young rider" is currently defined as one being under twenty-six years of age on January 1 of the year following the Tour. The competition might appear to be no more than a marketing gimmick dreamed up by the organisers, but in fact, the white jersey has always served as a very good indicator of future potential. The first "youngster" to win the competition was the Italian cyclist Francesco Moser, who finished seventh in the final general classification. He went on to enjoy a glittering career, dominating the classics from the mid-1970s to the early 1980s and winning the 1984 Giro d'Italia.

A select four riders have reached Paris with both the *maillot jaune* and the *maillot blanc*: Laurent Fignon in 1983, Jan Ullrich in 1997, Alberto Contador in 2007 and Andy Schleck in 2010. Just three riders have achieved multiple wins. Ullrich and Schleck each won three times: Ullrich in 1996, 1997 and 1998 and Schleck in 2008, 2009 and 2010. Marco Pantani won the competition twice, in 1994 and 1995. Greg LeMond tasted white jersey victory just once, in 1984, but he did go on to win the Tour three times. As for Nairo Quintana, the Colombian has the honour of being the only rider to have won both the white and polka dot jerseys in the same year, 2013.

Finally, special mention must go to the late Laurent Fignon (1960-2010), gone too soon — he was precocious in everything. In 1983, Bernard Hinault was unable to start the Tour, owing to knee problems, leaving the Renault-Elf team leaderless until a 22-year-old Fignon stepped into the breach. He remained a discreet presence for the first week, but managed to cross the Pyrenees alongside the top riders. By the end of stage ten, from Pau to Bagnères de Luchon, he had worked his way up to second place in the general classification, behind Pascal Simon. The next day, Simon was involved in a crash, fracturing his shoulder blade. He struggled on for several more stages, but the pain eventually became too much and he was forced to withdraw from the race at the end of stage sixteen, having hauled himself to the top of Alpe d'Huez. The next evening, Fignon found himself in yellow. And just in case anyone doubted that the youngster merited the *maillot jaune*, he won the penultimate stage, a time trial, in Dijon. Fignon proved that when it comes to the Tour de France, the fire of youth can be just as potent as age and experience. ■

TOUR DE FRANCE 1983
Laurent Fignon (left) ended up taking the white and yellow jerseys, after Pascal Simon (right) gave up the *maillot jaune* when he abandoned the race during stage 17 to Alpe d'Huez.

TOUR DE FRANCE 1975
The Italian rider Francesco Moser
won the first white jersey competition
of the Grande Boucle.

FINAL WINNERS
OF THE WHITE JERSEY

1975 Francesco Moser (ITA)
1976 Enrique Martínez Heredia (ESP)
1977 Dietrich Thurau (GER)
1978 Henk Lubberding (LUX)
1979 Jean-René Bernaudeau (FRA)
1980 Johan van der Velde (NED)
1981 Peter Winnen (NED)
1982 Phil Anderson (AUS)
1983 Laurent Fignon (FRA)
1984 Greg LeMond (USA)
1985 Fabio Parra (COL)
1986 Andrew Hampsten (USA)
1987 Raúl Alcalá (MEX)
1988 Erik Breukink (NED)
1989 Fabrice Philipot (FRA)
1990 Gilles Delion (FRA)
1991 Álvaro Mejía (COL)
1992 Eddy Bouwmans (NED)
1993 Antonio Martín Velasco (ESP)
1994 Marco Pantani (ITA)
1995 Marco Pantani (ITA)
1996 Jan Ullrich (GER)
1997 Jan Ullrich (GER)
1998 Jan Ullrich (GER)
1999 Benoît Salmon (FRA)
2000 Francisco Mancebo (ESP)
2001 Óscar Sevilla (ESP)
2002 Ivan Basso (ITA)
2003 Denis Menchov (RUS)
2004 Vladimir Karpets (RUS)
2005 Yaroslav Popovych (UKR)
2006 Damiano Cunego (ITA)
2007 Alberto Contador (ESP)
2008 Andy Schleck (LUX)
2009 Andy Schleck (LUX)
2010 Andy Schleck (LUX)
2011 Pierre Rolland (FRA)
2012 Tejay van Garderen (USA)
2013 Nairo Quintana (COL)
2014 Thibault Pinot (FRA)

Alexandre Geniez
leads Cyril Gautier and
Wilco Kelderman towards
his hometown of Rodez,
but the peloton would
swallow up the breakaway
within sight of the line.

GREG VAN AVERMAET, THE POWER AND THE GLORY

An undulating *parcours*, a steep uphill finish and searing heat — as the Tour raced from the Pyrenees to the Alps, on the first of four transitional stages, this certainly wasn't the restorative day out some in the peloton must have been hoping for. Six riders escaped in an early breakaway: Thomas De Gendt and Wilco Kelderman, the attacking rouleurs of Lotto-Soudal and Lotto-Jumbo; Nathan Haas, riding his first Tour, for Cannondale; Pierre-Luc Périchon of Bretagne-Séché; Europcar's Cyril Gautier; and Alexandre Geniez of FDJ, dreaming of a win in his native Rodez. Six riders representing six teams and no threat to the GC — they were hoping for clemency from the pack. But the pack had other ideas. The sprinters, after three days toiling on alien terrain, were hungry for action, and within a few kilometres John Degenkolb's Giant-Alpecin had organised the chase.

The temperature was knocking on 40 °C as the six rode on, collaborating well, but never gaining more than five minutes over the peloton. As the hills rose around them, Tinkoff-Saxo joined the chase, working for Peter Sagan and hoping for something more than second place. 64 km from the finish, AG2R's Monsieur Unlucky, Jean-Christophe Péraud, clipped a wheel and fell heavily, skinning his left side, and ripping his shorts beyond the point of modesty. His left arm totally covered in blood, he remounted, had his wounds dressed by the race doctor, and managed to regain the peloton, even collecting *bidons* for his teammates on the way.

By the time the breakaway was ten kilometres from the finish, only Gautier, De Gendt and Kelderman remained, with the peloton just forty-five seconds behind. What

> *"200 metres from the line, I felt someone on my wheel. When I saw it was Sagan, I just hoped he wouldn't manage to overtake."*
>
> **GREG VAN AVERMAET**

played out was a perfect demonstration of Chapatte's Law, named after the celebrated French cyclist and sports journalist, Robert Chapatte. He developed the rule of thumb that a peloton chasing a breakaway will gain one minute every ten kilometres. Sure enough, by the time the brave trio reached the *flamme rouge*, the peloton was bearing down, finally swallowing them an excruciating 300 metres from the line. For his efforts, De Gendt was named the day's most aggressive rider.

On paper, the last sharp kick uphill suited Sagan to perfection. He jumped after Greg Van Avermaet, whose own mammoth effort had dislodged the other sprinters. But just as he reached Van Avermaet's wheel, instead of going past, Sagan sat down, and the Flemish rider powered away to claim BMC's third stage win of the Tour. Seven seconds behind, the favourites finished together. As for Sagan, he was less than happy placing second for the fourth time this Tour, but could console himself with what was starting to look like an unassailable lead in the fight for the green jersey. ■

CLASSIFICATION FOR STAGE 13

1. VAN AVERMAET Greg (BEL, BMC) 4h43'42"
2. Sagan P (SVK, Tinkoff-Saxo) +0"
3. Bakelants J (BEL, AG2R La Mondiale) +3"
4. Degenkolb J (GER, Giant-Alpecin) +7"
5. Martens P (GER, LottoNL-Jumbo) +7"
6. Froome C (GBR, SKY) +7"
7. Nibali V (ITA, Astana) +7"
8. Contador A (ESP, Tinkoff-Saxo) +7"
9. Valverde A (ESP, Movistar) +7"
10. van Garderen T (USA, BMC) +7"
11. Gallopin T (FRA, Lotto-Soudal) +7"
12. Quintana N (COL, Movistar) +7"
13. Gesink R (NED, LottoNL-Jumbo) +7"
14. Thomas G (GBR, Sky) +7"
15. Štybar Z (CZE, Etixx – Quick-Step) +17"

Winner's average speed: 42 km/h

GENERAL CLASSIFICATION

1. FROOME Christopher (GBR, Sky) 51h34'21"
2. van Garderen T (USA, BMC) +2'52"
3. Quintana N (COL, Movistar) +3'09"
4. Valverde A (ESP, Movistar) +3'58"
5. Thomas G (GBR, Sky) +4'03"
6. Contador A (ESP, Tinkoff-Saxo) +4'04"
7. Gesink R (NED, LottoNL-Jumbo) +5'32"
8. Gallopin T (FRA, Lotto-Soudal) +7'32"
9. Nibali V (ITA, Astana) +7'47"
10. Mollema B (NED, Trek) +8'02"
11. Barguil W (FRA, Giant-Alpecin) +9'53"
12. Frank M (SUI, IAM) +12'35"
13. Sánchez S (ESP, BMC) +13'14"
14. Rolland P (FRA, Europcar) +14'07"
15. Bardet R (FRA, AG2R La Mondiale) +17'26"

FROOME C (GBR, SKY)

SAGAN P (SVK, TINKOFF-SAXO)

FROOME C (GBR, SKY)
worn by Rodríguez J (ESP, Katusha)

QUINTANA N (COL, MOVISTAR)

Team classification

MOVISTAR TEAM:
156h04'17"

MOST AGGRESSIVE RIDER
DE GENDT T (BEL, LOTTO-SOUDAL)

An aggrieved Peter Sagan sees victory slip away yet again. Greg Van Avermaet is triumphant as he savours his first ever stage win in the Tour de France.

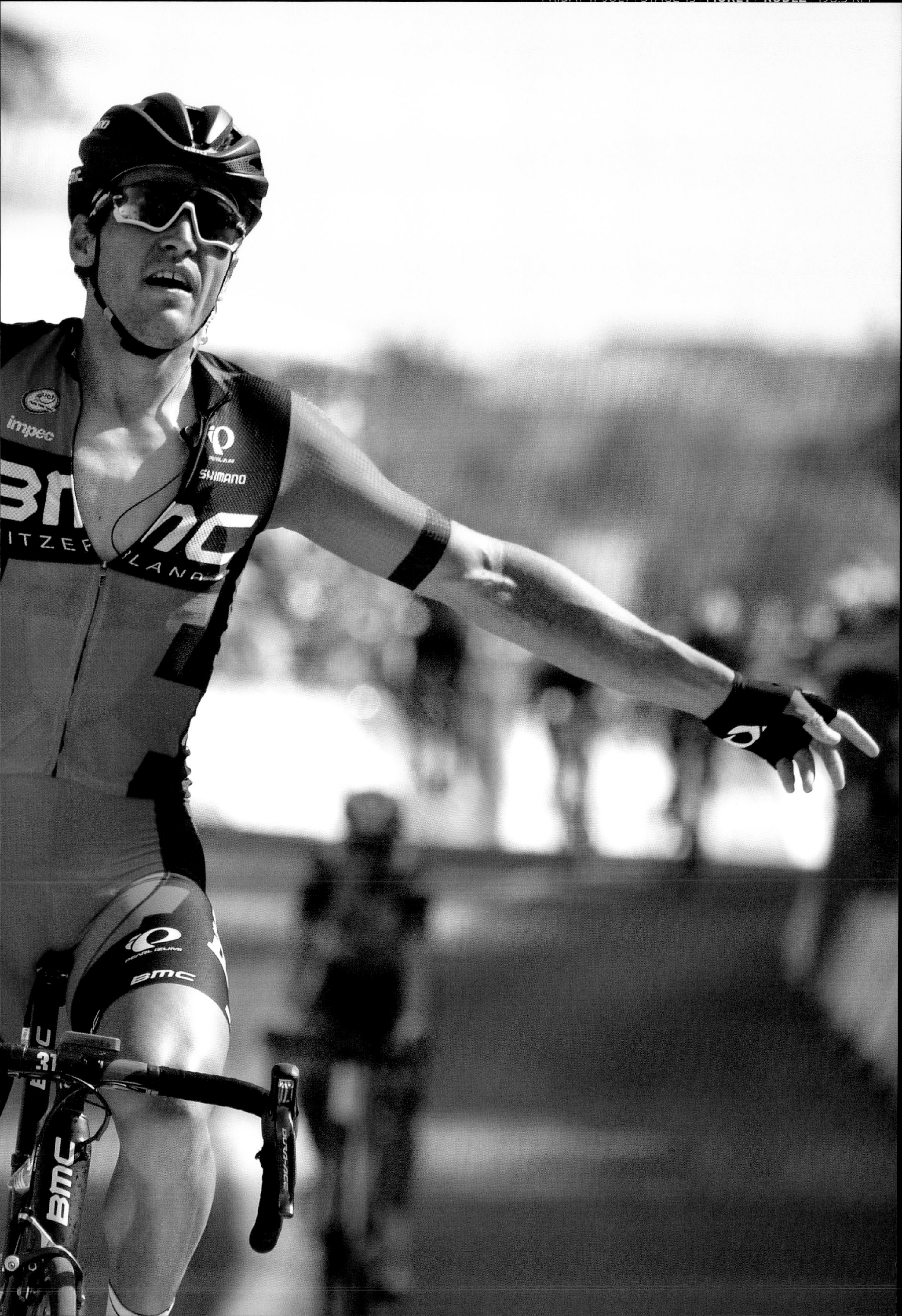
impec
SHIMANO
BMC

Tucked low for maximum
aerodynamic efficiency,
Steve Cummings swoops past
Pinot and Bardet, setting
himself up for a decisive victory.

STEVE CUMMINGS, SHREWD AND CLASSY

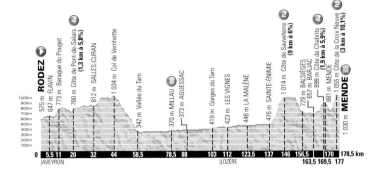

The road to Côte de la Croix Neuve had become something of a favourite on the Tour. The steep 3 km climb is known in cycling circles as Montée Laurent Jalabert, after the French former pro who won there on Bastille Day in 1995. But today, despite their best efforts, the French would not rule the mountain.

Stage fourteen was perfectly set for an early breakaway to go the distance: a long, hilly course, with hardly any flat stretches, and the final climb of the Côte de la Croix Neuve, finishing on the runway of the Mende Aerodrome. After the intermediate sprint at Millau, two breakaway groups merged into one, which included Romain Bardet, Thibaut Pinot and Steve Cummings, as well as Simon Yates, Rigoberto Urán and the irrepressible Peter Sagan. FDJ, who had three men in the break, did much of the pacemaking to set things up for Pinot. The peloton, marshalled by Team Sky, never chased seriously to catch them, but made sure they didn't take too much time.

The leading group began to disintegrate as it hit the foot of the final climb, and Kristijan Koren and Michał Golas were able to grab a few seconds' lead. But they were soon caught and passed by Bardet, who quickly opened up a gap, and when Pinot made the junction, the finale looked set to be a duel between the two young Frenchmen. What they hadn't reckoned on was a lone British rider spoiling the party. Steve Cummings is a cyclist with a rich experience riding pursuit on the track with the Great Britain cycling team, but he also has a solid road racing pedigree. He caught Pinot and Bardet just after the summit, and before they even realised, had flown past them. Throwing his bike through the last right-hand bend and onto the final straight, Cummings used a combination of momentum and pure grit to hold them off until the line — it was a fine demonstration of how a track man wins a race.

Back down the road, other skirmishes were playing out, with possible repercussions on the GC. Froome was isolated early on the final climb, and Quintana seized the opportunity to attack. The yellow jersey responded immediately, catching and then shadowing the Colombian, and even having the strength to outsprint him to the line, gaining just a single second, but also dealing a psychological blow. Nevertheless, Quintana's strong showing earned him second spot in the GC, and sent a message that his fight for yellow was in no way over.

Meanwhile, celebrations were well underway for Steve Cummings and MTN-Qhubeka. What better way for the wildcard South African team to mark Mandela Day, than with their first stage win in the Tour de France. ∎

> *"The last few years, I thought I was capable of doing this, and I just needed to find the right team to give me the opportunity."*
>
> **STEVE CUMMINGS**

CLASSIFICATION FOR STAGE 14

1. CUMMINGS Stephen (GBR, MTN-Qhubeka) 4h23'43"
2. Pinot T (FRA, FDJ) +2"
3. Bardet R (FRA, AG2R La Mondiale) +3"
4. Urán R (COL, Etixx – Quick-Step) +20"
5. Sagan P (SVK, Tinkoff-Saxo) +29"
6. Gautier C (FRA, Europcar) +32"
7. Plaza R (ESP, Lampre-Merida) +32"
8. Jungels B (LUX, Trek) +32"
9. Castroviejo J (ESP, Movistar) +32"
10. Yates S (GBR, Orica-GreenEdge) +33"
11. Bakelants J (BEL, AG2R La Mondiale) +1'07"
12. Pantano J (COL, IAM) +1'10"
13. Périchon P-L (FRA, Bretagne-Séché) +2'
14. Koren K (SVK, Cannondale-Garmin) +2'12"
15. de Kort K (NED, Giant-Alpecin) +2'12"

Winner's average speed: 40.6 km/h
Did not start: Morabito S (SUI, FDJ), Sinkeldam R (NED, Giant-Alpecin)
Disqualified: Sepúlveda E (ARG, Bretagne-Séché)

GENERAL CLASSIFICATION

1. FROOME Christopher (GBR, Sky) 56h02'19"
2. Quintana N (COL, Movistar) +3'10"
3. van Garderen T (USA, BMC) +3'32"
4. Valverde A (ESP, Movistar) +4'02"
5. Contador A (ESP, Tinkoff-Saxo) +4'23"
6. Thomas G (GBR, Sky) +4'54"
7. Gesink R (NED, LottoNL-Jumbo) +6'23"
8. Nibali V (ITA, Astana) +8'17"
9. Gallopin T (FRA, Lotto-Soudal) +8'23"
10. Mollema B (NED, Trek) +8'53"
11. Barguil W (FRA, Giant-Alpecin) +11'03"
12. Bardet R (FRA, AG2R La Mondiale) +13'10"
13. Frank M (SUI, IAM) +13'26"
14. Sánchez S (ESP, BMC) +14'21"
15. Rolland P (FRA, Europcar) +14'58"

FROOME C (GBR, SKY)

SAGAN P (SVK, TINKOFF-SAXO)

FROOME C (GBR, SKY)
worn by Rodríguez J (ESP, Katusha)

QUINTANA N (COL, MOVISTAR)

Team classification

MOVISTAR TEAM: 169h24'33"

MOST AGGRESSIVE RIDER
PÉRICHON P-L (FRA, BRETAGNE-SÉCHÉ)

The riders have no time to marvel at the spectacular geology of the Gorges du Tarn, as they race towards Mende.

(Top) At the top of the Côte de la Croix Neuve, Pinot and Bardet are unaware that Cummings is bearing down on them. Having failed to cooperate, they are now condemned to share defeat. (Bottom) Quintana appears in rude health as he attacks on the final climb. But Froome would keep his cool, and pass him on the finishing straight.

Contador and Valverde make their way up the Côte de la Croix Neuve, each in his own style. While Contador suffers, a comfortable Valverde looks to be in good form.

Katusha drive a hard pace to reel in the breakaway, but in the end, their man Alexander Kristoff would only finish third in Valence.

ANDRÉ GREIPEL MAKES IT A HAT-TRICK

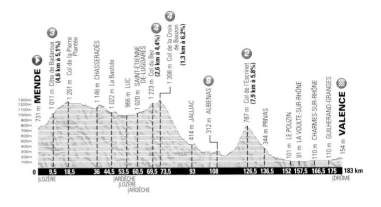

The *parcours* of the 2015 Tour had not been kind to the fast men, and this was the last stage before the Champs-Élysées in which they stood a serious chance of taking a win. The mission was clear for those teams with an interest in a sprint finish: chase down the breakaways, and bring their turbocharged specialists safely to the front of the bunch by the time it swept beneath the *flamme rouge*.

There were lots of tired and battered bodies in the peloton. After three exhausting days in the Pyrenees, and two almost as tiring transitional days, the *autobus* contained such notables as Mark Cavendish, suffering an upset stomach, and Jean-Christophe Péraud, recuperating after his crash on stage thirteen.

Peter Sagan, still seeking to bag a stage win, made sure he was in the early breakaway. He pushed a hard pace, determined not to let this opportunity slip away. The breakaway started to shed men, reducing to a solid bunch of nine riders comprising Adam Yates, Thibaut Pinot, who was keen to get over the previous day's humiliation, Ryder Hesjedal, Michael Rogers, Lars Bak, Simon Geschke, Michał Kwiatkowski and Matteo Trentin. After climbing the Col de Bez at kilometre 69.5, they had a two-minute advantage on the peloton, which grew to three minutes by kilometre 95. At the intermediate sprint in Aubenas, Sagan went away to pocket twenty precious points.

Back in the peloton, a hard pace was being set by Katusha, who were looking out for their sprinter, Alexander Kristoff, and by Europcar, who were betting on Bryan Coquard. Trentin and Hesjedal attacked off the front of the breakaway, but were caught 30 km from the line, their erstwhile companions having been gobbled up by the peloton 10 km back. A mass sprint seemed like a foregone conclusion. Suddenly, with 3.5 km to go, a rider propelled himself out of the peloton. It was stage six winner Zdeněk Štybar, his lead-out duties suspended now that teammate Mark Cavendish was languishing in the *autobus*. A desperate peloton hurled itself after "Štyby", who looked like he was going to land a second victory. But by the time the *flamme rouge* came into sight, he knew he didn't have the legs to go all the way, and sat up. The lead-out men of Lotto-Soudal, Katusha and Europcar whipped past, sprinters poised in their slipstreams. On the line, it was a photo finish: Greipel, then Degenkolb, then Kristoff, who had been lacking that extra kick since the start of the Tour. The GC contenders finished safely in the bunch, with no change in the standings.

The Gorilla savoured his third victory since Utrecht, and his ninth in five Tours. Sagan was frustrated in fourth but secured his grip on the green jersey, and Cavendish survived, hoping to recover in time for the next round. Now, all that stood between the sprinters and their final showdown, was the Alps. ∎

> ## "I'm really proud of the team, and of myself too. We really finished it off today."
> **ANDRÉ GREIPEL**

CLASSIFICATION FOR STAGE 15

1. GREIPEL André (GER, Lotto-Soudal)
   3h56'35"
2. Degenkolb J (GER, Giant-Alpecin) +0"
3. Kristoff A (NOR, Katusha) +0"
4. Sagan P (SVK, Tinkoff-Saxo) +0"
5. Boasson Hagen E (NOR, MTN-Qhubeka) +0"
6. Navardauskas R (LIT, Cannondale-Garmin) +0"
7. Laporte C (FRA, Cofidis) +0"
8. Matthews M (AUS, Orica-GreenEdge) +0"
9. Cimolai D (ITA, Lampre-Merida) +0"
10. Vachon F (FRA, Bretagne-Séché) +0"
11. Pantano J (COL, IAM) +0"
12. Bakelants J (BEL, AG2R La Mondiale) +0"
13. Voss P (GER, Bora-Argon 18) +0"
14. Martens P (GER, LottoNL-Jumbo) +0"
15. Coquard B (FRA, Europcar) +0"

Winner's average speed: 46.4 km/h

Did not finish: Langeveld S (NED, Cannondale-Garmin)

GENERAL CLASSIFICATION

1. FROOME Christopher (GBR, Sky)
   59h58'54"
2. Quintana N (COL, Movistar) +3'10"
3. van Garderen T (USA, BMC) +3'32"
4. Valverde A (ESP, Movistar) +4'02"
5. Contador A (ESP, Tinkoff-Saxo) +4'23"
6. Thomas G (GBR, Sky) +4'54"
7. Gesink R (NED, LottoNL-Jumbo) +6'23"
8. Nibali V (ITA, Astana) +8'17"
9. Gallopin T (FRA, Lotto-Soudal) +8'23"
10. Mollema B (NED, Trek) +8'53"
11. Barguil W (FRA, Giant-Alpecin) +11'03"
12. Bardet R (FRA, AG2R La Mondiale) +13'10"
13. Frank M (SUI, IAM) +13'26"
14. Sánchez S (ESP, BMC) +14'21"
15. Rolland P (FRA, Europcar) +14'58"

FROOME C (GBR, SKY)

SAGAN P (SVK, TINKOFF-SAXO)

FROOME C (GBR, SKY)
worn by Rodríguez J (ESP, Katusha)

QUINTANA N (COL, MOVISTAR)

Team classification

MOVISTAR TEAM:
181h14'18"

MOST AGGRESSIVE RIDER
SAGAN P (SVK, TINKOFF-SAXO)

A close sprint in Valence. From left to right: Peter Sagan (4th), Alexander Kristoff (3rd), John Degenkolb (2nd) and André Greipel, taking his third win.

Having switched to Lampre at the start of the season to support Rui Costa, who abandoned the race on stage eleven, Rubén Plaza knew when to take his chance.

RUBÉN PLAZA, DESCENT TO VICTORY

This long day provided two races for the price of one: the first, a nail-biting struggle for stage victory; the second, a tense chase to close GC time gaps. Attacks came thick and fast from the start. Twenty-nine riders finally made it clear, and soon split into two groups. Prominent in the first was Peter Sagan, whose presence in the bunch was probably not appreciated. The other riders knew they wouldn't stand a chance of beating him to the line unless they dropped him before the finishing straight, and that would be a tall order. Unlike other sprinters, Sagan relishes this kind of undulating terrain.

At the Col de Cabre, the breakaway had opened up a gap of 13 minutes on the peloton. Sagan barrelled into the descent at full tilt, which endeared him even less to his breakaway companions. 50 km from the finish, they began to attack him in earnest, but he doggedly chased each one down. 10 km further on, Adam Hansen and Marco Haller finally managed to break free, only to be pulled back on the last climb of the day, the second-category Col de Manse. There came another flurry of unsuccessful attacks, until, 3 km from the summit, Rubén Plaza made the decisive move. This time, Sagan couldn't follow.

The perilous descent from the Col de Manse is infamous in Tour history. It was here, in 2003, that Joseba Beloki's career effectively came to an end when he skidded on a patch of melted tar and was thrown off the bike, breaking his femur, elbow and wrist. This year, it nearly robbed Chris Froome of his trusty lieutenant, Geraint Thomas. Warren Barguil braked too late into a bend and careened into the Welshman, sending him flying headfirst into a telegraph pole and then down the steep, forested bank. There were sighs of relief all round as Thomas rode into view at the finish, safely on the wheel of teammate Wouter Poels, having lost only 38 seconds and his favourite sunglasses.

At the front of the race, Rubén Plaza began his descent of the Col de Manse with a 50 second gap on Sagan, one of the best bike handlers in the peloton. The Slovak gave a master class in the art of descending, pulling back 20 seconds, but it wasn't enough — the Spaniard held out to cross the line 30 seconds clear, taking the biggest win of his career.

A quarter of an hour behind, race two was heating up. The peloton was nearing the final climb when first Contador then Nibali went on the attack to try and steal time from Froome. Contador was soon reeled in, but the 2014 Tour champion was able to claw his way off the front, taking 28 seconds from his rivals at the finish. He may still have been 7'49" behind the *maillot jaune*, but, psychologically, that half-minute would have been invaluable to him. As for Froome, he would enjoy the second rest day knowing that his nearest rival, Nairo Quintana, was over three minutes in arrears. ■

> *"I knew Sagan was gaining on me, but I had a lead of fifty seconds at the summit, enough that I didn't panic."*
>
> **RUBÉN PLAZA**

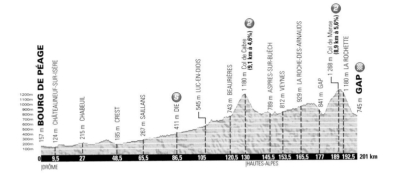

CLASSIFICATION FOR STAGE 16

1. PLAZA Rubén (ESP, Lampre-Merida) 4h30'10"
2. Sagan P (SVK, Tinkoff-Saxo) +30"
3. Pantano J (COL, IAM) +36"
4. Geschke S (GER, Giant-Alpecin) +40"
5. Jungels B (LUX, Trek) +40"
6. Riblon C (FRA, AG2R La Mondiale) +40"
7. Teklehaimanot D (ERI, MTN-Qhubeka) +53"
8. De Gendt T (BEL, Lotto-Soudal) +1'
9. Maté L Á (ESP, Cofidis) +1'22"
10. Voeckler T (FRA, Europcar) +1'22"
11. Fédrigo P (FRA, Bretagne-Séché) +1'54"
12. Grivko A (UKR, Astana) +1'54"
13. Pauwels S (BEL, MTN-Qhubeka) +1'54"
14. Golas M (POL, Etixx – Quick-Step) +1'55"
15. Erviti I (ESP, Movistar) +2'19"

Winner's average speed: 44.6 km/h
Did not start: Van Avermaet G (BEL, BMC)
Did not finish: Kennaugh P (GBR, Sky)

GENERAL CLASSIFICATION

1. FROOME Christopher (GBR, Sky) 64h47'16"
2. Quintana N (COL, Movistar) +3'10"
3. van Garderen T (USA, BMC) +3'32"
4. Valverde A (ESP, Movistar) +4'02"
5. Contador A (ESP, Tinkoff-Saxo) +4'23"
6. Thomas G (GBR, Sky) +5'32"
7. Gesink R (NED, LottoNL-Jumbo) +6'23"
8. Nibali V (ITA, Astana) +7'49"
9. Mollema B (NED, Trek) +8'53"
10. Barguil W (FRA, Giant-Alpecin) +11'03"
11. Gallopin T (FRA, Lotto-Soudal) +12'02"
12. Bardet R (FRA, AG2R La Mondiale) +13'10"
13. Frank M (SUI, IAM) +14'23"
14. Sánchez S (ESP, BMC) +15'18"
15. Rolland P (FRA, Europcar) +15'55"

FROOME C (GBR, SKY)

SAGAN P (SVK, TINKOFF-SAXO)

FROOME C (GBR, SKY)
worn by Rodríguez J (ESP, KATUSHA)

QUINTANA N (COL, MOVISTAR)

Team classification

MOVISTAR TEAM:
195h23'31"

MOST AGGRESSIVE RIDER
SAGAN P (SVK, TINKOFF-SAXO)

Finishing second for the fifth time, but named the day's most aggressive rider, Peter Sagan has poured his heart and soul into this year's Tour.

These lucky spectators watch the peloton speed past in a blur of jerseys.

(Top) Strung out in
a long line, the peloton
enjoys some welcome
shade on a baking
hot day.
(Bottom) The fearsome
Alps rise majestically
in the distance.

THE TOUR CARAVAN

The Tour de France caravan is a unique sight, rousing the enthusiasm of some ten million spectators thanks to its 156 festive vehicles and 14 million goodies.

1. The magical images captured by France Télévisions are beamed to 190 countries.
2. His Serene Highness Willem-Alexander, King of the Netherlands.
3. Jan van Zanen, the mayor of Utrecht, prepares to wave the start flag for the 2015 Tour.
4. His Majesty King Philippe of Belgium at the start of stage four (Seraing to Cambrai).
5. The actor Eddie Peng is the new Tour de France ambassador to China.
6. Bernard Hinault smiles as the French Prime Minister Manuel Valls congratulates Chris Froome after stage twelve (Lannemezan to Plateau de Beille).
7. The French President François Hollande was the guest of honour of Tour de France Director Christian Prudhomme on stage fourteen (Rodez to Mende).

Simon Geschke's epic escape led to his first Tour victory, at the summit of Pra-Loup.

SIMON GESCHKE, MOUNTAIN MAN

There are those who bemoan modern cycling, a world obsessed with comparative performance indicators and power output curves. They cast a nostalgic gaze back to a not-so-distant past when man attacked mountain with nothing but a steel bicycle and true grit; when the only data available were the time-gaps shouted by spectators with stopwatches. They would say that Bernard Thévenet's devouring of the The Cannibal, Eddy Merckx, on the overheated slopes of Pra-Loup in 1975 was a case in point. Thévenet would win the Tour. Merckx would never wear yellow again.

Yet despite the power meters and the squawking radios, the most important ingredient is as present as ever — courage. The courage to ignore the data, to ride on instinct, to attack. The courage of riders like Peter Sagan, Thibaut Pinot and Giant-Alpecin's Simon Geschke, who gave Germany its fifth victory of this Tour.

Early in the stage, there was a flurry of attacks in an attempt to establish a breakaway. Nothing stuck, and it was only on the ascent of the Col de Toutes Aures that a group of twenty-eight riders escaped, including Geschke, Sagan and Pinot.

Battling desperately to keep his third place in the GC was Tejay van Garderen. Sick and suffering, he was dropped on the day's first climb. He dug deep and rode himself back, but couldn't stand the pace on the ascent to the Col de la Colle-Saint-Michel. 91 kilometres into the stage, he abandoned. 20 kilometres up the road, Michał Kwiatkowski, wearing the rainbow stripes of world champion, also climbed off, his tank empty. He sat, dejected, by the side of the road, while his *directeur sportif* shouted at him.

With little cooperation in the breakaway, Simon Geschke took his chance and attacked on the lower slopes of the Col d'Allos, building a lead of two minutes. Pinot set off in pursuit, and had closed to within a minute by the time Geschke went over the summit. But Pinot is no Sagan when it comes to descending. He skidded and fell coming out of a bend, and although he swiftly remounted, the incident rattled him and caution took hold. Talansky passed him, then Urán. Geschke, meanwhile, churned away up the final, 6 km climb to Pra-Loup. Talansky gained on him, but was still 32 seconds adrift when Geschke crossed the line — his courageous attack had paid off.

Seven minutes back, the favourites cautiously marked each other, with Team Sky shutting down any moves against their leader. On the descent of the Col d'Allos, Contador crashed and lost a significant 2'17". A few hundred metres from the finish, Quintana launched a late attack, perhaps a statement of intent for the days to come. Froome was able to counter, and the two gapped Nibali and Valverde by just a few more seconds.

As the Tour enters its final stages, the challengers have no lack of technology at their disposal, but they will need all the courage they can muster. ∎

> *"Today, I was the breakaway."*
> **SIMON GESCHKE**

CLASSIFICATION FOR STAGE 17

1. GESCHKE Simon (GER, Giant-Alpecin) 4h12'17"
2. Talansky A (USA, Cannondale-Garmin) +32"
3. Urán R (COL, Etixx – Quick-Step) +1'01"
4. Pinot T (FRA, FDJ) +1'36"
5. Mathias F (SUI, IAM) +1'40"
6. Kruijswijk S (NED, LottoNL-Jumbo) +2'27"
7. Roche N (IRL, Sky) +3'02"
8. Castroviejo J (ESP, Movistar) +3'04"
9. Pauwels S (BEL, MTN-Qhubeka) +3'05"
10. Yates A (GBR, Orica-GreenEdge) +3'21"
11. Bakelants J (BEL, AG2R La Mondiale) +4'26"
12. Teklehaimanot D (ERI, MTN-Qhubeka) +4'50"
13. Majka R (POL, Tinkoff-Saxo) +4'54"
14. Kudus M (ERI, MTN-Qhubeka) +5'55"
15. Hesjedal R (CAN, Cannondale-Garmin) +5'58"

Winner's average speed: 38.3 km/h
Did not start: Didier L (LUX, Trek)
Did not finish: van Garderen T (USA, BMC), Kwiatkowski M (POL, Etixx – Quick-Step), Haas N (AUS, Cannondale-Garmin), Coppel J (FRA, IAM), Bennett S (IRL, Bora-Argon 18)

GENERAL CLASSIFICATION

1. FROOME Christopher (GBR, Sky) 69h06'49"
2. Quintana N (COL, Movistar) +3'10"
3. Valverde A (ESP, Movistar) +4'09"
4. Thomas G (GBR, Sky) +6'34"
5. Contador A (ESP, Tinkoff-Saxo) +6'40"
6. Gesink R (NED, LottoNL-Jumbo) +7'39"
7. Nibali V (ITA, Astana) +8'04"
8. Frank M (SUI, IAM) +8'47"
9. Mollema B (NED, Trek) +11'47"
10. Barguil W (FRA, Giant-Alpecin) +13'08"
11. Bardet R (FRA, AG2R La Mondiale) +16'04"
12. Talansky A (USA, Cannondale-Garmin) +16'25"
13. Sánchez S (ESP, BMC) +17'52"
14. Rolland P (FRA, Europcar) +18'37"
15. Pauwels S (BEL, MTN-Qhubeka) +20'07"

FROOME C (GBR, SKY)

SAGAN P (SVK, TINKOFF-SAXO)

FROOME C (GBR, SKY)
worn by Rodríguez J (ESP, Katusha)

QUINTANA N (COL, MOVISTAR)

MOVISTAR TEAM:
208h18'05"

MOST AGGRESSIVE RIDER
GESCHKE S (GER, GIANT-ALPECIN)

Nibali, Froome, Quintana, Valverde and Contador stay glued to each other up the Col d'Allos. For several days, the battle for the podium has been taking place behind the fight for the stage win.

KINGS OF THE MOUNTAINS

The mountains classification has existed since 1933, when its first winner was the Spanish rider, Vicente Trueba. However, it wasn't until 1975 that the polka dot jersey for the leader of this competition was introduced, along with the white jersey for the best young rider.

Mountain stages are the very heart of the Tour de France. Not only is overall victory virtually unachievable without a consistently strong showing on this terrain, but also the long, brutal climbs are where virtuoso cyclists have pulled off some of the most staggering stage wins. Iconic names forever linked to the Tour's equally iconic ascents include Gino Bartali, Fausto Coppi, Charly Gaul, Federico Bahamontes, Julio Jiménez and, of course, Lucien Van Impe, the first man to wear the polka dot jersey and six-times winner of the mountains classification.

In the mid 1980s it was the Colombians, most notably Luis "Lucho" Herrera, who ruled the mountains. Weighing in at a featherweight 57 kg and with his ability to glide up the steepest of gradients, "Lucho" was a pure climber. In 1985, stage fourteen from Autrans-Méaudre to Saint-Étienne saw him go toe-to-toe with Bernard Hinault on the ascent to Avoriaz. "Lucho" rode to victory, and wore the polka dot jersey all the way to Paris, becoming the first Colombian to win the mountains classification. He won this again in 1987, and indeed was crowned "King of the Mountains" in all three grand tours during his career.

The record for most wins in the mountains classification is held by Richard Virenque, a worthy heir to such great French climbers as René Vietto, Jean Dotto, Nello Lauredi and Lucien Lazaridès. Virenque won the competition a total of seven times, including four consecutive titles from 1994 to 1997. Following the 1998 Festina doping scandal and his disciplinary suspension, he returned to win the competition a further three times, in 1999, 2003 and 2004.

Virenque's first taste of the *maillot a pois* came in 1992, after the second stage from San Sebastián to Pau, where he also picked up the yellow, green and white jerseys — although he lost them all by the time the Tour reached Paris. But the 1994 Tour was where he made good on that early promise. He won the twelfth stage, from Lourdes to Luz Ardiden, taking the polka dot jersey, and this time keeping it for the rest of Tour. As well as winning the mountains classification, the Frenchman ranked an impressive fifth in the general classification. In 1997, when "Virenquemania" was at its height, he won the twelfth stage from Bourg d'Oisans to Courchevel in spectacular style. Five years later, when he was making his comeback, Virenque conquered the formidable Mont Ventoux after a long solo breakaway. It was his fifth — and perhaps most beautiful — Tour de France stage victory. Bastille Day 2004 saw him play the national hero by winning stage ten from Limoges to Saint-Flour in the Massif Central — a final taste of Olympus before hanging up his wheels for good. ■

TOUR DE FRANCE 1975
Under the guidance of the shrewd Cyrille Guimard, Lucien Van Impe wore the inaugural polka dot jersey on the way to the third of his six mountains competition wins.

FINAL WINNERS OF THE POLKA DOT JERSEY

1975	Lucien Van Impe (BEL)
1976	Giancarlo Bellini (ITA)
1977	Lucien Van Impe (BEL)
1978	Mariano Martínez (FRA)
1979	Giovanni Battaglin (ITA)
1980	Raymond Martin (FRA)
1981	Lucien Van Impe (BEL)
1982	Bernard Vallet (FRA)
1983	Lucien Van Impe (BEL)
1984	Robert Millar (GBR)
1985	Luis Herrera (COL)
1986	Bernard Hinault (FRA)
1987	Luis Herrera (COL)
1988	Steven Rooks (NED)
1989	Gert-Jan Theunisse (NED)
1990	Thierry Claveyrolat (FRA)
1991	Claudio Chiappucci (ITA)
1992	Claudio Chiappucci (ITA)
1993	Tony Rominger (SUI)
1994	Richard Virenque (FRA)
1995	Richard Virenque (FRA)
1996	Richard Virenque (FRA)
1997	Richard Virenque (FRA)
1998	Christophe Rinero (FRA)
1999	Richard Virenque (FRA)
2000	Santiago Botero (COL)
2001	Laurent Jalabert (FRA)
2002	Laurent Jalabert (FRA)
2003	Richard Virenque (FRA)
2004	Richard Virenque (FRA)
2005	Michael Rasmussen (DEN)
2006	Michael Rasmussen (DEN)
2007	Mauricio Soler (COL)
2008	Carlos Sastre (ESP)
2009	Egoi Martínez (ESP)
2010	Anthony Charteau (FRA)
2011	Samuel Sánchez (ESP)
2012	Thomas Voeckler (FRA)
2013	Nairo Quintana (COL)
2014	Rafał Majka (POL)

Romain Bardet dances on the pedals as he rides towards an epic stage victory in Saint-Jean de Maurienne.

ROMAIN BARDET, CHAMPION IN THE MAKING

This second Alpine stage contained two major set-pieces: the mighty Col du Glandon and, making a Tour debut, the eighteen hairpins of the Lacets de Montvernier, cresting 6 km from the finish. All along the route, throngs of expectant French supporters eagerly hoped for another home victory, following Vuillermoz's success on stage eight.

The peloton had just completed the first climb of the day, the Col de Bayard, when Tour Radio announced the formation of a large breakaway containing a strong contingent of French riders, namely Bardet, Riblon, Pinot, Rolland, Gautier, Sicard and Voeckler. Also in the break was Joaquim Rodríguez, polka dot jersey wearer by proxy, but aiming to win it in his own right.

The battle burst into life four kilometres from the summit of the Col du Glandon, when the breakaway, now reduced to eleven men, broke apart in the wake of a strong attack from Pierre Rolland. Anacona, Bardet and Fuglsang were the only riders able to follow. The Dane crashed and Rolland cracked, leaving Bardet and Anacona to crest over the Glandon in the lead. The long descent was fast and technical, which suited Bardet perfectly, and he soon outpaced his companion, hurtling downhill in a reprise of his winning performance in the Pra-Loup stage of the Critérium du Dauphiné a month before.

At the foot of the Lacets de Montvernier, with Bardet enjoying a 47 second lead on the chasing group, and with victory seemingly in his sights, Europcar rider Gautier laid down a hammering pace for his team leader Pierre Rolland, in an attempt to close the gap. But the AG2R rider didn't falter, his pedalling smooth and steady. Rolland worked hard to catch him, but Bardet rode solo to the line with a lead of 33 seconds, a beautiful victory, and his first in the Tour de France. His efforts saw him move up to tenth place in the GC, second place in the young rider classification and joint first place with Rodríguez in the mountains classification — although it was the Spaniard who donned the polka dot jersey again that evening, his combined points having come from higher rated climbs.

Froome retained his overall lead, and all the main contenders finished together. Despite Contador making an attack on the Glandon that saw him open up a lead of nearly a minute on the other favourites, the hard yet steady pace set by Geraint Thomas closed the gap before the top of the climb. Nibali and Quintana also tried a couple of jabs, but they either didn't have the legs or else were saving themselves for the queen stage the next day.

It is thirty years since Bernard Hinault became France's last Tour de France champion. For many people, the young Romain Bardet represents the shining future of French cycling, a potential heir to The Badger's crown. ■

> *"Losing at Mende has made me a winner today."*
> **ROMAIN BARDET**

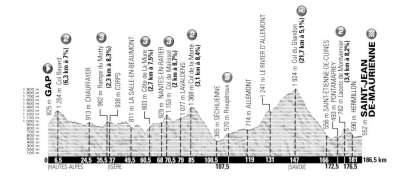

CLASSIFICATION FOR STAGE 18

1. BARDET Romain (FRA, AG2R La Mondiale) 5h03'40"
2. Rolland P (FRA, Europcar) +33"
3. Anacona W (COL, Movistar) +59"
4. Jungels B (LUX, Trek) +59"
5. Fuglsang J (DEN, Astana) +59"
6. Pauwels S (BEL, MTN-Qhubeka) +1'01"
7. Gautier C (FRA, Europcar) +1'50"
8. Caruso D (ITA, BMC) +1'50"
9. Talansky A (USA, Cannondale-Garmin) +1'55"
10. Barguil W (FRA, Giant-Alpecin) +3'02"
11. Gesink R (NED, LottoNL-Jumbo) +3'02"
12. Froome C (GBR, Sky) +3'02"
13. Valverde A (ESP, Movistar) +3'02"
14. Thomas G (GBR, Sky) +3'02"
15. Contador A (ESP, Tinkoff-Saxo) +3'02"

GENERAL CLASSIFICATION

1. FROOME Christopher (GBR, Sky) 74h13'31"
2. Quintana N (COL, Movistar) +3'10"
3. Valverde A (ESP, Movistar) +4'09"
4. Thomas G (GBR, Sky) +6'34"
5. Contador A (ESP, Tinkoff-Saxo) +6'40"
6. Gesink R (NED, LottoNL-Jumbo) +7'39"
7. Nibali V (ITA, Astana) +8'04"
8. Frank M (SUI, IAM) +8'47"
9. Mollema B (NED, Trek) +12'06"
10. Bardet R (FRA, AG2R La Mondiale) +12'52"
11. Barguil W (FRA, Giant-Alpecin) +13'08"
12. Talansky A (USA, Cannondale-Garmin) +15'18"
13. Rolland P (FRA, Europcar) +16'02"
14. Pauwels S (BEL, MTN-Qhubeka) +18'06"
15. Sánchez S (ESP, BMC) +18'11"

Winner's average speed: 36.8 km/h
Did not start: Meintjes L (RSA, MTN-Qhubeka)
Did not finish: Renshaw M (AUS, Etixx – Quick-Step)

FROOME C (GBR, SKY)

SAGAN P (SVK, TINKOFF-SAXO)

RODRÍGUEZ J (ESP, KATUSHA)

QUINTANA N (COL, MOVISTAR)

Team classification

MOVISTAR TEAM:
223h36'08"

MOST AGGRESSIVE RIDER
BARDET R (FRA, AG2R LA MONDIALE)

(Top) The magnificently named Winner Anacona is on the rivet as Romain Bardet blasts up the Glandon. (Bottom) The chasing group climbs through a sea of spectators.

Pierre Rolland swore
he would give it his
all in the Alps,
and he did just that.

The breathtaking beauty of the Lacets de Montvernier would be Romain Bardet's stairway to glory.

Once a champion, always a champion. A determined Vincenzo Nibali reminds everyone that he's one of the best bike riders in the world.

VINCENZO NIBALI, THE SHARK ATTACKS

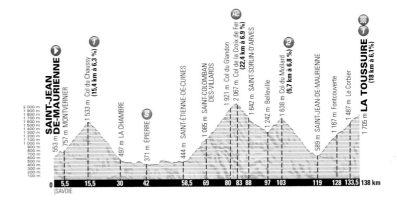

The queen stage of the 2015 Tour de France lived up to its billing. Even before the top of the first climb — the first-category Col du Chaussy — attacks from Contador, Valverde and Nibali left Chris Froome isolated, his Sky team scattered along the mountain road. They managed to regroup on the descent, but that rare show of weakness was a boon for the other challengers.

Joaquim Rodríguez led over the top of the climb, chased by Bardet, Urán and Rolland, among others. The group coalesced into a solid breakaway of twenty-two riders, as it sped along the valley floor towards the mighty Col de la Croix de Fer. As the escape group fragmented on the ascent, Pierre Rolland attacked, in search of a second win at La Toussuire, after his victory there in 2012.

The tough slopes of the Col de la Croix de Fer also shattered the peloton. Geraint Thomas, Chris Froome's right-hand man, lost touch with the leaders and wouldn't recover, ultimately dropping from fourth to fifteenth place in the GC. As the remainders of the *maillot jaune* group approached the summit, Froome had to pull up and clear a stone that had jammed in his brakes. At the same moment, Nibali looked back towards the yellow jersey, and then attacked. Whether he saw Froome stop, or not, is debatable, but his return to form was beyond doubt as he climbed away from the leaders.

By the time Rolland began his descent of the Col du Mollard, Nibali was just eight seconds behind. The Italian gave a conspiratorial pat on the back as he caught Rolland, and they forged on together. Romain Bardet was chasing hard, but developed a problem with his front derailleur and so couldn't turn a big enough gear to catch them. Nibali and Rolland began the 18 km ascent to La Toussuire, but whatever pact they had made was declared null and void when Nibali rode away 16 km from the finish. The "Shark of Messina" went on to take the stage win at the summit of La Toussuire.

Back in the yellow jersey group, things seemed relatively calm until Quintana went on the offensive, 6 km from the finish. For perhaps the first time this Tour, an isolated Froome was unable to follow, and Quintana managed to put a 30 second dent in his lead.

A brave Bardet finished fifth, pocketing just enough points to pass Rodríguez and take the lead in the mountains classification, along with the honour of wearing the polka dot jersey up Alpe d'Huez the next day. As for Nibali, his *tour de force* had taken him into fourth place in the GC, saving his Tour, and perhaps even making the podium in Paris a possibility. Quintana didn't quite get the gap on Froome he needed, but showed again that he is the better climber on this Tour.

Cycling's greatest climb, the Alpe d'Huez, would be a fitting arena for the Tour's decisive stage. ∎

> *"I don't know what will happen tomorrow, with all the energy I've spent today."*
>
> **VINCENZO NIBALI**

CLASSIFICATION FOR STAGE 19

1. NIBALI Vincenzo (ITA, Astana) 4h22'53"
2. Quintana N (COL, Movistar) +44"
3. Froome C (GBR, Sky) +1'14"
4. Pinot T (FRA, FDJ) +2'26"
5. Bardet R (FRA, AG2R La Mondiale) +2'26"
6. Valverde A (ESP, Movistar) +2'26"
7. Mollema B (NED, Trek) +2'26"
8. Gesink R (NED, LottoNL-Jumbo) +2'26"
9. Contador A (ESP, Tinkoff-Saxo) +2'26"
10. Sánchez S (ESP, BMC) +2'26"
11. Rolland P (FRA, Europcar) +2'35"
12. Talansky A (USA, Cannondale-Garmin) +4'17"
13. Plaza R (ESP, Lampre-Merida) +4'53"
14. Frank M (SUI, IAM) +5'02"
15. Majka R (POL, Tinkoff-Saxo) +5'02"

Winner's average speed: 31.5 km/h
Did not finish: Valgren M (DEN, Tinkoff-Saxo)

GENERAL CLASSIFICATION

1. FROOME Christopher (GBR, Sky) 78h37'34"
2. Quintana N (COL, Movistar) +2'38"
3. Valverde A (ESP, Movistar) +5'25"
4. Nibali V (ITA, Astana) +6'44"
5. Contador A (ESP, Tinkoff-Saxo) +7'56"
6. Gesink R (NED, LottoNL-Jumbo) +8'55"
7. Frank M (SUI, IAM) +12'39"
8. Mollema B (NED, Trek) +13'22"
9. Bardet R (FRA, AG2R La Mondiale) +14'08"
10. Rolland P (FRA, Europcar) +17'27"
11. Talansky A (USA, Cannondale-Garmin) +18'25"
12. Sánchez S (ESP, BMC) +19'27"
13. Pauwels S (BEL, MTN-Qhubeka) +26'48"
14. Barguil W (FRA, Giant-Alpecin) +27'00"
15. Thomas G (GBR, Sky) +27'24"

FROOME C (GBR, SKY)

SAGAN P (SVK, TINKOFF-SAXO)

BARDET R (FRA, AG2R LA MONDIALE)

QUINTANA N (COL, MOVISTAR)

Team classification
MOVISTAR TEAM:
236h58'50"

MOST AGGRESSIVE RIDER
ROLLAND P (FRA, EUROPCAR)

The art of descending.
(Left) Rolland: efficiency,
at all costs.
(Top) Nibali: audacious,
but always the right line.
(Bottom) Bardet: more
traditional, but just
as effective.

6 km from the finish, Quintana demonstrates his climbing supremacy as he pulls away from Froome.

Thibaut Pinot gives a magnificent display of climbing prowess on the slopes of Alpe d'Huez, to crown three weeks of bad luck and injury and enter into Tour legend.

THIBAUT PINOT, A LEGEND ON THE ALPE

Three hard weeks of racing, over a *parcours* unlike any the Tour de France has known, led to this, the ascent of the legendary Alpe d'Huez one day before the finish in Paris. A final, epic chance for riders to achieve their ambitions, or at least lay their demons to rest.

Once again, breakaway attempts began as soon as the starting flag was lowered. FDJ man Alexandre Geniez escaped and was joined by Ramūnas Navardauskas, Lars Bak and Nicolas Edet. 6 km from the summit of the *hors catégorie* Col de la Croix de Fer, Geniez launched the solo attack he would carry onto the upper slopes of Alpe d'Huez.

Meanwhile, on the slopes of the Croix de Fer, the GC fireworks began. Valverde launched the first salvo of a tactical volley for Movistar, a classic one-two that was completed 1 km up the road, when Quintana jumped from the bunch to join him. Despite having none of his teammates at hand, Froome managed to hold the Movistar duo at no more than 15", a small enough gap to bridge on the long descent, and allow the yellow jersey group to reform.

Geniez commenced his ascent of the Alpe, closely pursued by a select group, among them Pinot, Anacona, Plaza, Serpa, Rolland and Hesjedal. Pinot joined his FDJ teammate 9 km from the summit, with Hesjedal on his wheel. But Geniez held on, and Pinot, displaying the talent that saw him place third in the 2014 Tour, dropped Hesjedal and climbed solo towards the finish. But he wasn't home free.

Further down the Alpe, hostilities had resumed. Nibali punctured at the foot of the climb, his chances of a podium finish deflated. Then, as the pace quickened, Contador raised the white flag. The remaining Sky *domestiques*, Poels and Porte, dug deep. All they needed to do was protect their leader and his lead — the end was in sight. Then Quintana attacked, and launched himself clear, making stepping stones of Valverde, then Anacona, and then fellow countryman José Serpa. For the second time this Tour, Froome looked in real difficulty, and just like before, it was Quintana applying the pressure.

The Colombian climber soloed on, giving it everything he had — chasing Pinot for the stage victory, and the now impossible time gap to the *maillot jaune*, he rode like a man possessed. But Pinot was equally motivated, and held out to cross the line, just 18" ahead.

Quintana managed to pull back 1'12" on Froome, over half his deficit in the GC, but it wasn't enough. The British rider suffered all the way to the line, securing his second Tour de France victory. And, despite Bardet's spirited efforts, Froome also took the mountains classification, meaning he will become the first rider since Eddy Merckx to win both the yellow and polka dot jerseys on the same Tour. As for stage winner Thibaut Pinot, bend fourteen will now forever bear his name. Alpe d'Huez: the mountain where legends are made. ∎

> *"Winning at Alpe d'Huez on the final stage is just extraordinary. I'm lost for words."*
> **THIBAUT PINOT**

CLASSIFICATION FOR STAGE 20

1. PINOT Thibaut (FRA, FDJ) 3h17'21"
2. Quintana N (COL, Movistar) +18"
3. Hesjedal R (CAN, Cannondale-Garmin) +41"
4. Valverde A (ESP, Movistar) +1'38"
5. Froome C (GBR, Sky) +1'38"
6. Rolland P (FRA, Europcar) +1'41"
7. Porte R (AUS, Sky) +2'11"
8. Anacona W (COL, Movistar) +2'32"
9. Poels W (NED, Sky) +2'50"
10. Plaza R (ESP, Lampre-Merida) +2'50"
11. Yates S (GBR, Orica-GreenEdge) +3'06"
12. Rodríguez J (ESP, Katusha) +3'12"
13. Jungels B (LUX, Trek) +3'26"
14. Mollema B (NED, Trek) +3'30"
15. Nibali V (ITA, Astana) +3'30"

Winner's average speed: 33.6 km/h

GENERAL CLASSIFICATION

1. FROOME Christopher (GBR, Sky) 81h56'33"
2. Quintana N (COL, Movistar) +1'12"
3. Valverde A (ESP, Movistar) +5'25"
4. Nibali V (ITA, Astana) +8'36"
5. Contador A (ESP, Tinkoff-Saxo) +9'48"
6. Gesink R (NED, LottoNL-Jumbo) +10'47"
7. Mollema B (NED, Trek) +15'14"
8. Frank M (SUI, IAM) +15'39"
9. Bardet R (FRA, AG2R La Mondiale) +16'
10. Rolland P (FRA, Europcar) +17'30"
11. Talansky A (USA, Cannondale-Garmin) +22'06"
12. Sánchez S (ESP, BMC) +22'50"
13. Pauwels S (BEL, MTN-Qhubeka) +31'03"
14. Barguil W (FRA, Giant-Alpecin) +31'15"
15. Thomas G (GBR, Sky) +31'39"

FROOME C (GBR, SKY)

SAGAN P (SVK, TINKOFF-SAXO)

FROOME C (GBR, SKY)
worn by Bardet R (FRA, AG2R La Mondiale)

QUINTANA N (COL, MOVISTAR)

Team classification

MOVISTAR TEAM:
246h55'21"

MOST AGGRESSIVE RIDER
GENIEZ A (FRA, FDJ)

(Top) Alexandre Geniez was named the day's Most Aggressive Rider for his long breakaway, serving as a relay for his leader Thibaut Pinot. (Bottom) There was a time when Alpe d'Huez belonged to the Dutch. But with Pierre Rolland winning in 2011, Christophe Riblon in 2013 and now Thibaut Pinot, it seems to be turning French again.

Nibali, Mollema, Majka and Contador grimace with the effort, as they pass Dutch Corner.

Quintana and Valverde make a joint attack, an effective tactic, but applied too late in the Tour to have a significant impact.

Battered but unbowed, Chris Froome sticks close to his loyal lieutenant Richie Porte.

FAUSTO COPPI, THE FIRST WINNER

In 1952, Jacques Goddet was looking to make the thirty-ninth Tour de France tougher than ever before. He decided the riders would ascend Alpe d'Huez, with its twenty-one formidable hairpins, culminating in the Tour's very first mountain-top finish.

The stage commenced in Lausanne, Switzerland, on Friday 4 July, with Fausto Coppi in fourth place overall and five minutes down. On reaching the Alpe, Jean Robic, the 1947 Tour champion, launched the kind of kamikaze move that was his trademark, attacking right at the foot of the climb. Coppi not only held on, he passed the Breton rider six kilometres from the top. It was an impressive performance. The Italian won the stage, beating Robic, who finished at 1'20", and the Belgian rider, Stan Ockers, at 3'22". What's more, when Coppi's great rival, the ageing Gino Bartali, reached the top, he was 5'21" behind the stage winner.

That evening, *Il Campionissimo* took the yellow jersey from his compatriot Andrea Carrea. All eyes were now on Coppi, and the next day's edition of *L'Équipe* ran a laudatory article by Claude Tillet declaring him to be "in a class of his own" and "the strongest man in the race". Tillet was right, and Coppi wore yellow all the way to Paris.

Despite the excitement that this brand new climb brought to the Tour, cycling fans had to wait twenty-four long years before Alpe d'Huez joined the pantheon of regular stage finishes. On July 4 1976, Joop Zoetemelk became the first in a string of Dutchmen to achieve glory on this iconic mountain top. Hennie Kuiper won there in 1977 and 1978. The following year, the Tour climbed the Alpe twice in forty-eight hours, with the Portuguese rider Joaquim Agostinho breaking the Dutch run by winning the first ascent, before Zoetemelk tasted victory again the next day. In 1981 and 1983, Peter Winnen claimed the Alpe, and in 1988, Steven Rooks took up the torch, which he handed to Gert-Jan Theunisse the following year.

A legend had been created, Alpe d'Huez was Dutch — at least as far as bike racing was concerned. The reality is that a Dutchman hasn't won here since 1989, a fact that hasn't dampened Dutch spirits. Bend No. 7, known as Dutch Corner, has become a place of pilgrimage, hosting an orange-clad army of fans from the Netherlands every time the tour tackles the Alpe. Still, with or without the Dutch, Alpe d'Huez's reputation as a legendary climb continues unabated. ■

TOUR DE FRANCE 1952
The Tour's first ever ascent of the Alpe d'Huez, and its first mountain-top finish, Fausto Coppi (right) passes Jean Robic (left), and would drop him 6 km from the summit. *Il Campionissimo* won the stage, at an average speed of 18.65 km/h, turning the Alpe into a legend.

TOUR DE FRANCE 1952
At the summit of Alpe d'Huez, Jean Masson, the French Minister for Youth and Sport, congratulates Fausto Coppi.

SUMMIT FINISHES AT ALPE D'HUEZ

1952 10th stage | Lausanne > Alpe d'Huez (266 km) | Winner: Fausto Coppi (ITA)
1952 9th stage | Divonne-les-Bains > Alpe d'Huez (258 km) | Winner: Joop Zoetemelk (NED)
1977 7th stage | Chamonix > Alpe d'Huez (184.5 km) | Winner: Hennie Kuiper (NED)
1978 16th stage | Saint-Étienne > Alpe d'Huez (240.5 km) | Winner: Hennie Kuiper (NED)
1979 17th stage | Les Menuires > Alpe d'Huez (166.5 km) | Winner: Joaquim Agostinho (POR)
1979 18th stage | Alpe d'Huez > Alpe d'Huez (118.5 km) | Winner: Joop Zoetemelk (NED)
1981 17th stage | Morzine > Alpe d'Huez (230.5 km) | Winner: Peter Winnen (NED)
1982 16th stage | Orcières-Merlette > Alpe d'Huez (123 km) | Winner: Beat Breu (SUI)
1983 17th stage | La Tour-du-Pin > Alpe d'Huez (223 km) | Winner: Peter Winnen (NED)
1984 17th stage | Grenoble > Alpe d'Huez (151 km) | Winner: Luis Herrera (COL)
1986 18th stage | Briançon > Alpe d'Huez (162.5 km) | Winner: Bernard Hinault (FRA)
1987 20th stage | Villard-de-Lans > Alpe d'Huez (201 km) | Winner: Federico Echave (ESP)
1988 12th stage | Morzine > Alpe d'Huez (227 km) | Winner: Steven Rooks (NED)
1989 17th stage | Briançon > Alpe d'Huez (165 km) | Winner: Gert-Jan Theunisse (NED)
1990 11th stage | Saint-Gervais > Alpe d'Huez (182.5 km) | Winner: Gianni Bugno (ITA)
1991 17th stage | Gap > Alpe d'Huez (125 km) | Winner: Gianni Bugno (ITA)
1992 14th stage | Sestrières > Alpe d'Huez (186.5 km) | Winner: Andrew Hampsten (USA)
1994 16th stage | Valréas > Alpe d'Huez (224.5 km) | Winner: Roberto Conti (ITA)
1995 10th stage | Aime > Alpe d'Huez (162.5 km) | Winner: Marco Pantani (ITA)
1997 13th stage | Saint-Étienne > Alpe d'Huez (203.5 km) | Winner: Marco Pantani (ITA)
1999 10th stage | Sestrières > Alpe d'Huez (220.5 km) | Winner: Giuseppe Guerini (ITA)
2001 10th stage | Aix-les-Bains > Alpe d'Huez (208 km) | Winner: Lance Armstrong (USA)
2003 8th stage | Sallanches > Alpe d'Huez (219 km) | Winner: Iban Mayo (ESP)
2004 16th stage | Le Bourg-d'Oisans > Alpe d'Huez (204 km) | Winner: Lance Armstrong (USA)
2006 15th stage | Gap > Alpe d'Huez (187 km) | Winner: Fränk Schleck (LUX)
2008 17th stage | Embrun > Alpe d'Huez (210.5 km) | Winner: Carlos Sastre (ESP)
2011 19th stage | Modane > Alpe d'Huez (109.5 km) | Winner: Pierre Rolland (FRA)
2013 18th stage | Gap > Alpe d'Huez (172.5 km) | Winner: Christophe Riblon (FRA)

As they climb 1,090 metres to the top of Alpe d'Huez, riders cover 13.8 km at an average gradient of 7.9%. The famous twenty-one hairpin bends are numbered, starting from twenty-one at the bottom, and each one is dedicated to a winner of the stage.

With Team Sky on the *pavé*, the *Patrouille de France* streaks overhead.

ANDRÉ GREIPEL, SIMPLY UNTOUCHABLE

How paradoxical that a Tour marked by baking heat should end beneath such inclement skies. The curtain of rain that swept across the final stage of the 2015 Tour de France was a reminder of the integral part that the weather plays in cycling. After three weeks of closely fought battles on perilous roads, the riders were hardly at serious risk, yet there was clear anxiety in a peloton that counted many wounded warriors in its ranks. With an eye on rider safety, the race organisers decided to record the final GC times on the first pass over the line on the Champs-Élysées — although every rider would still have to complete the stage — and the first couple of circuits of the Champs-Élysées, usually a blur of wheels and jerseys, were positively sedate.

In past editions of the Tour, particularly during the Merckx-Thévenet years, the Champs-Élysées witnessed fierce battles for final placing in the general classification. But for the past decade, at least, convention has dictated that riders observe an open truce, leaving the way clear for the sprinters or tough older warriors. Men such as Jens Voigt and David Millar, or today's attacking rider, Sylvain Chavanel.

Eventually, the rain cleared, and a light breeze dried the slick *pavé*, confirming, if there was ever any doubt, that a sprint showdown would provide the Tour's final dénouement. There were many sprinters eager for victory at the end of a race *parcours* that had not been kind to them. French riders like Démare, Coquard and Soupe, and others such as Kristoff, Sagan, Cavendish and of course the German fast men, Degenkolb and the dominant André Greipel. So despite Chavanel's 7 km solo breakaway, and attempts by Oliveira, Vanbilsen, Vachon, and stage one winner, Rohan Dennis, the peloton regrouped 5 km from the finish. It was all over in a flash; Kristoff led the sprint, but faded with 200 meters to go as Greipel blasted by, just edging out Coquard, whose bike throw was so forceful, his front wheel left the ground as he crossed the line.

It was a breathtaking end to a gripping race. Greipel claimed his fourth stage win of the Tour, Sagan won his fourth Green jersey competition, Quintana wore white and stood second on the podium for the second time in his career, and Chris Froome sealed the deal on both the *maillot jaune* and the polka dot jersey. He had suffered in the way only a champion can, parrying attacks from his valiant opponents in the peloton, his critics in the press, and, unfortunately, from the occasional hooligan on the roadside. But Froome rose to every challenge, becoming the first British rider to win the Tour de France twice, and the ultimate victor of one of the greatest editions of the *Grande Boucle* ever raced. ∎

> *"I've claimed the biggest success of my career on the Champs-Élysées, in the capital of the sprint."*
>
> **ANDRÉ GREIPEL**

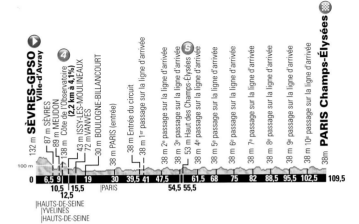

CLASSIFICATION FOR STAGE 21

1. GREIPEL André (GER, Lotto-Soudal) 2h49'41"
2. Coquard B (FRA, Europcar) +0"
3. Kristoff A (NOR, Katusha) +0"
4. Boasson Hagen E (NOR, MTN-Qhubeka) +0"
5. Démare A (FRA, FDJ) +0"
6. Cavendish M (GBR, Etixx – Quick-Step) +0"
7. Sagan P (SVK, Tinkoff-Saxo) +0"
8. Degenkolb J (GER, Giant-Alpecin) +0"
9. Matthews M (AUS, Orica-GreenEdge) +0"
10. Navardauskas R (LIT, Cannondale-Garmin) +0"
11. Trentin M (ITA, Etixx – Quick-Step) +0"
12. Laporte C (FRA, Cofidis) +0"
13. Soupe G (FRA, Cofidis) +0"
14. Vanmarcke S (BEL, LottoNL-Jumbo) +0"
15. Pantano J (COL, IAM) +0"

Winner's average speed: 38.7 km/h

GENERAL CLASSIFICATION

1. FROOME Christopher (GBR, Sky) 84h46'14"
2. Quintana N (COL, Movistar) +1'12"
3. Valverde A (ESP, Movistar) +5'25"
4. Nibali V (ITA, Astana) +8'36"
5. Contador A (ESP, Tinkoff-Saxo) +9'48"
6. Gesink R (NED, LottoNL-Jumbo) +10'47"
7. Mollema B (NED, Trek) +15'14"
8. Frank M (SUI, IAM) +15'39"
9. Bardet R (FRA, AG2R La Mondiale) +16'
10. Rolland P (FRA, Europcar) +17'30"
11. Talansky A (USA, Cannondale-Garmin) +22'06"
12. Sánchez S (ESP, BMC) +22'50"
13. Pauwels S (BEL, MTN-Qhubeka) +31'03"
14. Barguil W (FRA, Giant-Alpecin) +31'15"
15. Thomas G (GBR, Sky) +31'39"

FROOME C (GBR, SKY)

SAGAN P (SVK, TINKOFF-SAXO)

FROOME C (GBR, SKY)

QUINTANA N (COL, MOVISTAR)

Team classification

MOVISTAR TEAM:
255h24'24"

André Greipel outsprints Alexander Kristoff, Peter Sagan, Edvald Boasson Hagen, Bryan Coquard and Arnaud Démare to take his fourth win in the 2015 Tour de France.

A cautious peloton veers round the Arc de Triomphe and onto the slick *pavé* of the Champs-Élysées.

(Top) Brothers in arms, Team Sky cross the line, resplendent in special edition yellow kit, celebrating Chris Froome's second Tour de France victory. (Bottom) Chris Froome stands on the podium, flanked by Nairo Quintana and Alejandro Valverde.

HOW THE TOUR FOUND ITS GRAND FINALE

The first Tour de France did not actually finish in Paris' Parc des Princes velodrome, as so many believe. Instead, thanks to a by-law that forbade bike racing inside the city limits, the final sprint took place in the small town of Ville-d'Avray, which lies between Paris and Versailles. Then, after a champagne celebration, the winner, Maurice Garin, and the nineteen other riders from the winning breakaway, cycled to Parc des Princes where they rode several laps of honour in front of an adoring crowd of 20,000 paying spectators.

Following the huge success of the first Tour, the offending by-law was repealed, and in 1904 the race's grand finale was indeed staged at Parc des Princes. So things would remain until 1967, the year Raymond Poulidor triumphed at the end of a final time trial, the last rider to win on the historic track. The roar of the fans had hardly died away when the demolition men began their work, closing one chapter in Tour history, but opening another.

The Tour organisers, Jacques Goddet and Félix Lévitan, searched for a new venue where the great race could play out its dramatic finale in front of a packed house.

The Tour's final stage saw the riders cycle twenty-five times round a circuit that began at Concorde, then ran alongside the Seine before returning via the Rue de Rivoli and onto the Champs-Élysées.

They chose a former Olympic velodrome in the Bois de Vincennes — La Cipale — and in 1968, the Dutch rider Jan Janssen was the first to be crowned Tour champion there. In 1987, La Cipale was renamed Vélodrome Jacques-Anquetil, in honour of the five-times Tour winner. But despite this, it will be forever associated with Eddy Merckx. The Cannibal sealed every one of his five victories here between 1969 and 1974, a run only interrupted by Luis Ocaña in 1973.

As the format of the Tour evolved, La Cipale ceased to be fit for purpose, despite its attractive setting. The journalist Yves Mourousi, with Félix Lévitan's approval, proposed that the Tour de France would find an epilogue worthy of its stature on the most beautiful avenue in the world, the Champs-Élysées. And so it was that in 1975, the Tour's final stage saw the riders cycle twenty-five times round a circuit that began at Concorde, then ran alongside the Seine before returning via the Rue de Rivoli and onto the Champs-Élysées. The 163.5 km stage was won by the great Belgian sprinter Walter Godefroot, with the Frenchman Bernard Thévenet taking top spot in the general classification. The French President, Valéry Giscard d'Estaing, whose support was decisive in getting the finish moved to such a prestigious location, presented Thévenet with the eighth of his sixteen career yellow jerseys and the first of his two Tour trophies.

For the 1976 Tour, the Champs-Élysées stage was split into two parts: a 6 km individual time trial in the morning and a 91 km mass-start stage in the afternoon. The time trial was won by Freddy Maertens, with Gerben Karstens taking victory in the afternoon. The format was repeated in 1977, this time with Dietrich Thurau winning against the clock and Alain Meslet becoming the first Frenchman to win a stage on the Champs-Élysées. Since 1978, the final stage has started in a town outside Paris, with the riders crossing the finish line several times as they race round the Champs-Élysées circuit.

TOUR DE FRANCE 1975
In this year of innovation, which also saw the introduction of the white and polka dot jerseys, the Tour finished on the Champs-Élysées for the very first time.

With the exception of a few rare breakaways, such as those by Alain Meslet in 1977, Eddy Seigneur in 1994 and Alexander Vinokourov in 2005, this stage is usually contested in a mass sprint. Mark Cavendish tops the leader board of Champs-Élysées wins, with four in succession, from 2009 to 2012, ahead of Bernard Hinault, who took two, in 1979 and 1982, as did the specialist sprinters Djamolidine Abdoujaparov (1993 and 1995), Robbie McEwen (1999 and 2002) and Marcel Kittel (2013 and 2014).

There's no doubt that the final stage on the Champs-Élysées has seen more than its fair share of drama over the last forty years. As far as heart-stopping moments go, Abdoujaparov might well top the bill for the terrifying crash that he suffered in 1991, although a close contender might be the incident during the rain-drenched 1977 finale, when Bernard Thévenet and Hennie Kuiper, top two in the general classification and separated by just forty-eight seconds, both crashed on the sixth circuit. In 1979, Bernard Hinault beat Joop Zoetemelk to the line in a gripping photo finish, a one-two that reflected their positions on the final podium. And in 1989, after an individual time trial, Greg Lemond snatched the yellow jersey and the race from Laurent Fignon by just eight seconds, the smallest winning margin ever recorded in the history of the Tour de France. ■

STAGE WINNERS ON THE CHAMPS-ÉLYSÉES

1975	Walter Godefroot (NED)	**1994**	Eddy Seigneur (FRA)
1976	Freddy Maertens (BEL, ITT);	**1995**	Djamolidine Abdoujaparov (UZB)
	Gerben Karstens (NED)	**1996**	Fabio Baldato (ITA)
1977	Dietrich Thurau (GER, ITT);	**1997**	Nicola Minali (ITA)
	Alain Meslet (FRA)	**1998**	Tom Steels (BEL)
1978	Gerrie Knetemann (NED)	**1999**	Robbie McEwen (AUS)
1979	Bernard Hinault (FRA)	**2000**	Stefano Zanini (ITA)
1980	Paul Verschuere (BEL)	**2001**	Ján Svorada (CZE)
1981	Freddy Maertens (BEL)	**2002**	Robbie McEwen (AUS)
1982	Bernard Hinault (FRA)	**2003**	Jean-Patrick Nazon (FRA)
1983	Gilbert Glaus (SUI)	**2004**	Tom Boonen (BEL)
1984	Eric Vanderaerden (BEL)	**2005**	Alexander Vinokourov (KAZ)
1985	Rudy Mathijs (BEL)	**2006**	Thor Hushovd (NOR)
1986	Guido Bontempi (ITA)	**2007**	Daniele Bennati (ITA)
1987	Jeff Pierce (USA)	**2008**	Gert Steegmans (BEL)
1988	Jean-Paul van Poppel (NED)	**2009**	Mark Cavendish (GBR)
1989	Greg LeMond (USA)	**2010**	Mark Cavendish (GBR)
1990	Johan Museeuw (BEL)	**2011**	Mark Cavendish (GBR)
1991	Dimitri Konyshev (USSR)	**2012**	Mark Cavendish (GBR)
1992	Olaf Ludwig (GER)	**2013**	Marcel Kittel (GER)
1993	Djamolidine Abdoujaparov (UZB)	**2014**	Marcel Kittel (GER)

TOUR DE FRANCE 1975
The Belgian rider Walter Godefroot wins the first stage finish on the Champs-Élysées, beating Frenchman Robert Mintkiewicz and Dutchman Gerben Karstens to the line in a mass sprint. British sprinter Barry Hoban, riding for Team Gan-Mercier, finished in fifth place.

FINAL CLASSIFICATIONS

GENERAL CLASSIFICATION

1. FROOME C (GBR, Sky) 84h46'14"
2. QUINTANA N (COL, Movistar) +1'12"
3. VALVERDE A (ESP, Movistar) +5'25"
4. NIBALI V (ITA, Astana) +8'36"
5. CONTADOR A (ESP, Tinkoff-Saxo) +9'48"
6. GESINK R (NED, LottoNL-Jumbo) +10'47"
7. MOLLEMA B (NED, Trek) +15'14"
8. FRANK M (SUI, IAM) +15'39"
9. BARDET R (FRA, AG2R La Mondiale) +16'00"
10. ROLLAND P (FRA, Europcar) +17'30"
11. TALANSKY A (USA, Cannondale-Garmin) +22'06"
12. SÁNCHEZ S (ESP, BMC) +22'50"
13. PAUWELS S (BEL, MTN-Qhubeka) +31'03"
14. BARGUIL W (FRA, Giant-Alpecin) +31'15"
15. THOMAS G (GBR, Sky) +31'39"
16. PINOT T (FRA, FDJ) +38'52"
17. KREUZIGER R (CZE, Tinkoff-Saxo) +1h02'51"
18. CHÉREL M (FRA, AG2R La Mondiale) +1h05'00"
19. PANTANO J (COL, IAM) +1h09'08"
20. BAKELANTS J (BEL, AG2R La Mondiale) +1h16'36"
21. KRUIJSWIJK S (NED, LottoNL-Jumbo) +1h21'27"
22. KANGERT T (EST, Astana) +1h24'58"
23. FUGLSANG J (DEN, Astana) +1h25'23"
24. CASTROVIEJO J (ESP, Movistar) +1h26'05"
25. BARTA J (CZE, Bora-Argon 18) +1h26'56"
26. VUILLERMOZ A (FRA, AG2R La Mondiale) +1h28'29"
27. JUNGELS B (LUX, Trek) +1h33'21"
28. MAJKA R (POL, Tinkoff-Saxo) +1h35'06"
29. RODRÍGUEZ J (ESP, Katusha) +1h36'07"
30. PLAZA R (ESP, Lampre-Merida) +1h38'22"
31. GALLOPIN T (FRA, Lotto-Soudal) +1h40'44"
32. IZAGIRRE G (ESP, Movistar) +1h41'34"
33. SICARD R (FRA, Europcar) +1h51'32"
34. GAUTIER C (FRA, Europcar) +1h51'51"
35. ROCHE N (IRL, Sky) +1h54'08"
36. ROGERS M (AUS, Tinkoff-Saxo) +1h56'13"
37. BAK L (DEN, Lotto-Soudal) +1h56'57"
38. GESCHKE S (GER, Giant-Alpecin) +1h58'14"
39. MARTIN D (IRL, Cannondale-Garmin) +2h03'37"
40. HESJEDAL R (CAN, Cannondale-Garmin) +2h04'37"
41. SCARPONI M (ITA, Astana) +2h05'03"
42. URÁN R (COL, Etixx – Quick-Step) +2h08'20"
43. MATÉ L Á (ESP, Cofidis) +2h10'12"
44. POELS W (NED, Sky) +2h12'44"
45. VOECKLER T (FRA, Europcar) +2h14'08"
46. SAGAN P (SVK, Tinkoff-Saxo) +2h14'55"
47. OLIVEIRA N (POR, Lampre-Merida) +2h15'32"
48. PORTE R (AUS, Sky) +2h16'05"
49. TEKLEHAIMANOT D (ERI, MTN-Qhubeka) +2h16'15"
50. YATES A (GBR, Orica-GreenEdge) +2h 16'36"
51. JANSE VAN RENSBURG J (RSA, MTN-Qhubeka) +2h18'16"
52. FÉDRIGO P (FRA, Bretagne-Séché) +2h22'54"
53. CARUSO D (ITA, BMC) +2h26'32"
54. CHAVANEL Sy (FRA, IAM) +2h29'28"
55. TANKINK B (NED, LottoNL-Jumbo) +2h30'12"
56. SCHÄR M (SUI, BMC) +2h31'13"
57. ANACONA W (COL, Movistar) +2h31'14"
58. LOSADA A (ESP, Katusha) +2h32'30"
59. CLEMENT S (NED, IAM) +2h33'42"
60. WYSS M (SUI, IAM) +2h34'38"
61. PÉRAUD J-C (FRA, AG2R La Mondiale) +2h35'10"
62. ZUBELDIA H (ESP, Trek) +2h36'50"
63. WYSS D (SUI, BMC) +2h37'17"
64. GRIVKO A (UKR, Astana) +2h38'06"
65. HERRADA J (ESP, Movistar) +2h40'06"
66. NAVARRO D (ESP, Cofidis) +2h43'34"
67. DE GENDT T (BEL, Lotto-Soudal) +2h48'02"

68. RIBLON C (FRA, AG2R La Mondiale) +2h48'19"
69. KOREN K (SVK, Cannondale-Garmin) +2h51'44"
70. KÖNIG L (CZE, Sky) +2h53'09"
71. LADAGNOUS M (FRA, FDJ) +2h53'22"
72. MACHADO T (POR, Katusha) +2h54'31"
73. DE KORT K (NED, Giant-Alpecin) +2h57'05"
74. QUÉMÉNEUR P (FRA, Europcar) +2h57'19"
75. HOLLENSTEIN R (SUI, IAM) +2h58'30"
76. ĐURASEK K (CRO, Lampre-Merida) +3h02'14"
77. WESTRA L (NED, Astana) +3h03'09"
78. VALLS R (ESP, Lampre-Merida) +3h03'11"
79. KELDERMAN W (NED, LottoNL-Jumbo) +3h04'07"
80. MARTENS P (GER, LottoNL-Jumbo) +3h04'52"
81. PÉRICHON P-L (FRA, Bretagne-Séché) +3h05'48"
82. BOASSON HAGEN E (NOR, MTN-Qhubeka) +3h08'02"
83. BUCHMANN E (GER, Bora-Argon 18) +3h08'47"
84. KUDUS GHEBREMEDHIN M (ERI, MTN-Qhubeka) +3h10'36"
85. DELAPLACE A (FRA, Bretagne-Séché) +3h11'28"
86. CUMMINGS S (GBR, MTN-Qhubeka) +3h12'23"
87. PREIDLER G (AUT, Giant-Alpecin) +3h14'14"
88. VACHON F (FRA, Bretagne-Séché) +3h15'01"
89. YATES S (GBR, Orica-GreenEdge) +3h16'04"
90. CARUSO G (ITA, Katusha) +3h17'03"
91. TULIK A (FRA, Europcar) +3h18'24"
92. TEN DAM L (NED, LottoNL-Jumbo) +3h18'43"
93. IRIZAR M (ESP, Trek) +3h19'44"
94. SIMON J (FRA, Cofidis) +3h19'53"
95. GOLAS M (POL, Etixx – Quick-Step) +3h21'17"
96. JANSE VAN RENSBURG R (RSA, MTN-Qhubeka) +3h21'30"
97. OSS D (ITA, BMC) +3h22'14"
98. FEILLU B (FRA, Bretagne-Séché) +3h23'11"
99. VOSS P (GER, Bora-Argon 18) +3h24'53"
100. ELMIGER M (SUI, IAM) +3h26'47
101. DENNIS R (AUS, BMC) +3h27'34"
102. RAST G (SUI, Trek) +3h29'00"
103. ŠTYBAR Z (CZE, Etixx – Quick-Step) +3h30'13"
104. VANMARCKE S (BEL, LottoNL-Jumbo) +3h31'15"
105. ROY J (FRA, FDJ) +3h32'12"
106. CURVERS R (NED, Giant-Alpecin) +3h35'40"
107. MALORI A (ITA, Movistar) +3h37'28"
108. HUZARSKI B (POL, Bora-Argon 18) +3h38'06"
109. DEGENKOLB J (GER, Giant-Alpecin) +3h39'43"
110. COQUARD B (FRA, Europcar) +3h42'36"
111. EDET N (FRA, Cofidis) +3h42'42"
112. GENIEZ A (FRA, FDJ) +3h42'57"
113. VAUGRENARD B (FRA, FDJ) +3h43'08"
114. HANSEN A (AUS, Lotto-Soudal) +3h45'18"
115. ERVITI I (ESP, Movistar) +3h47'14"
116. VERMOTE J (BEL, Etixx – Quick-Step) +3h50'32"
117. TRENTIN M (ITA, Etixx – Quick-Step) +3h50'59"
118. BONO M (ITA, Lampre-Merida) +3h52'17"
119. FONSECA A (FRA, Bretagne-Séché) +3h53'13"
120. QUINZIATO M (ITA, BMC) +3h53'21"
121. VAN EMDEN J (NED, LottoNL-Jumbo) +3h54'19"
122. SERPA J (COL, Lampre-Merida) +3h54'25"
123. SOUPE G (FRA, Cofidis) +3h55'35"
124. ARREDONDO J (COL, Trek) +3h56'49"
125. POZZATO F (ITA, Lampre-Merida) +3h58'20"
126. HALLER M (AUT, Katusha) +3h59'04"
127. LAPORTE C (FRA, Cofidis) +3h59'10"
128. STANNARD I (GBR, Sky) +3h59'37"
129. WELLENS T (BEL, Lotto-Soudal) +3h59'39"
130. KRISTOFF A (NOR, Katusha) +4h01'06"
131. GRUZDEV D (KAZ, Astana) +4h01'12"
132. TOSATTO M (ITA, Tinkoff-Saxo) +4h01'15"
133. GÉRARD A (FRA, Bretagne-Séché) +4h02'06"
134. GREIPEL A (GER, Lotto-Soudal) +4h03'28"

135. SÉNÉCHAL F (FRA, Cofidis) +4h04'06"
136. ROWE L (GBR, Sky) +4h04'45"
137. GÈNE Y (FRA, Europcar) +4h04'56"
138. DÉMARE A (FRA, FDJ) +4h05'28"
139. TIMMER A (NED, Giant-Alpecin) +4h05'30"
140. PIMANTA J (POR, Bora-Argon 18) +4h07'47"
141. BRUN F (FRA, Bretagne-Séché) +4h10'32"
142. CAVENDISH M (GBR, Etixx – Quick-Step) +4h12'05"
143. NAVARDAUSKAS R (LIT, Cannondale-Garmin) +4h14'40"
144. WEENING P (NED, Orica-GreenEdge) +4h15'20"
145. DEBUSSCHERE J (BEL, Lotto-Soudal) +4h16'06"
146. GAUDIN D (FRA, AG2R La Mondiale) +4h16'13"
147. VAN BAARLE D (NED, Cannondale-Garmin) +4h18'40"
148. DEVOLDER S (BEL, Trek) +4h21'31"
149. GUARNIERI J (ITA, Katusha) +4h22'20"
150. SIEBERG M (GER, Lotto-Soudal) +4h24'52"
151. DURBRIDGE L (AUS, Orica-GreenEdge) +4h25'03"
152. MATTHEWS M (AUS, Orica-GreenEdge) +4h26'33"
153. LEEZER T (NED, LottoNL-Jumbo) +4h26'47"
154. FARRAR T (USA, MTN-Qhubeka) +4h32'32"
155. CIMOLAI D (ITA, Lampre-Merida) +4h33'21"
156. BRÄNDLE M (AUT, IAM) +4h37'36"
157. NAULLEAU B (FRA, Europcar) +4h40'12"
158. VANBILSEN K (BEL, Cofidis) +4h41'27"
159. TUFT S (CAN, Orica-GreenEdge) +4h48'08"
160. CHAVANEL Sé (FRA, FDJ), +4h56'59"

POINTS CLASSIFICATION

1. SAGAN P (SVK, Tinkoff-Saxo) 432 pts
2. GREIPEL A (GER, Lotto-Soudal) 366 pts
3. DEGENKOLB J (GER, Giant-Alpecin) 298 pts
4. CAVENDISH M (GBR, Etixx – Quick-Step) 206 pts
5. COQUARD B (FRA, Europcar) 152 pts

MOUNTAINS CLASSIFICATION

1. FROOME C (GBR, Sky) 119 pts
2. QUINTANA N (COL, Movistar) 108 pts
3. BARDET R (FRA, AG2R La Mondiale) 90 pts
4. PINOT T (FRA, FDJ) 82 pts
5. RODRÍGUEZ J (ESP, Katusha) 78 pts

YOUNG RIDER CLASSIFICATION

1. QUINTANA N (COL, Movistar) 84h47'26"
2. BARDET R (FRA, AG2R La Mondiale) +14'48"
3. BARGUIL W (FRA, Giant-Alpecin) +30'03"
4. PINOT T (FRA, FDJ) +37'40"
5. JUNGELS B (LUX, Trek) +1h32'09"

TEAM CLASSIFICATION

1. MOVISTAR TEAM (ESP) 255h24'24"
2. TEAM SKY (GBR) +57'23"
3. TINKOFF-SAXO (RUS) +1h00'12"
4. ASTANA PRO TEAM (KAZ) +1h12'09"
5. MTN-QHUBEKA (RSA) +1h14'32"

MOST AGGRESSIVE RIDER

BARDET R (FRA, AG2R La Mondiale)

PHOTOGRAPHIC CREDITS

All photographs in this book were provided by the Presse Sports agency (Boué, Deschamps, Mantey, Mons, Papon, Prévost, Sunada), except for the images on pages 100-103 and 143 (top left and right, centre left and right): © A.S.O. (Bade, Bourgois, Demouveaux, Perreve).

Produced for Vision Sports Publishing by Copyright Éditions
Image editing: Cédric Delsart and emigreen
Production: Stéphanie Parlange and Cédric Delsart

Printed in Spain, August 2015